HOLGER SPAMANN

CORPORATIONS

CORPORATIONS

By Holger Spamann

Independently published on KDP.

COLOPHON

The serif font used in this book is EQUITY.

The sans serif font is CONCOURSE.

Both were designed by Matthew Butterick.

ISBN-13: 978-1790591626

Second Edition, December 2018.

About This Book

This book is a print edition of materials created and made available by Holger Spamann on H2O, an online learning and content platform. The online version, including access to the full text of the cases presented herein, is available at https://opencasebook.org/casebooks/79342-corporations.

A few notes on the book's formatting:

1. Original source materials, including cases, are presented in san serif font, e.g.:

    "Two cases pitting the directors of Atlas Corporation against that company's largest (9.1%) shareholder, Blasius Industries, have been consolidated and tried together."

2. Footnotes in san serif font are taken from the original case.

3. Materials written by the author are presented in serif font, e.g.:

    "Formally speaking, a corporation is nothing but an abstraction to which we assign rights and duties."

4. Additional notes or annotations by the author appear in several formats in the text. Some are included as footnotes, in serif font. Others are inline comments, in which case they presented in grey and generally preceded by the author's initials, e.g., [HS: The buyer could then merge with Transunion]. Others are presented as sidenotes, also in grey, with the location to which they refer marked with a diamond, e.g., ◆.

    ◆ Example of a sidenote.

5. Elided text—parts of cases that have been removed by the author—is indicated by [...]. In several cases, text has been removed and replaced with abbreviated summaries, which is indicated with [bracketed serif text].

Contents

Author's Note

I designed this book as the basis for a first course in corporate law. Besides the usual cases and other excerpted materials, the book contains extensive introductions and explanations that I wrote specifically for this book. Instructors considering adopting this book should contact me for additional materials, particularly quizzes and case studies, that I use in my class.

Compared to standard casebooks, I use fewer cases, but I edit them sparingly and sometimes not at all. One reason for this is that the number of seminal cases in corporate law is small. I believe you are better served by knowing the important cases well, rather than by skimming a lot of less important cases. Additionally, much of corporate law consists of broad standards that take on real meaning only in their application. That is why understanding the law often requires reading the full facts of the opinion. The judges clearly considered these factual details important, even on appeal, and so should you! The other reason for focusing on fewer cases is that I want to give you the time necessary to understand the underlying business scenarios, and to reflect on the interactions of the rules discussed in the cases. In corporate law, this is not easy. The structures and transactions are often complex. Please try to understand them as best you can.

I have organized the materials largely around the doctrine and particular corporate events. But any one case involves multiple issues, including the underlying business issues. You will learn better if you try to understand the full case, rather than zooming in narrowly on the headline doctrine.

With one exception, all of the cases in these materials are either Delaware or federal cases. Delaware law is the dominant corporate law of the United States. In the U.S., each state has its own corporate law, and the applicable law is the law of the state of incorporation. Corporations are free to incorporate where they want, in return for paying incorporation tax ("franchise tax") in that jurisdiction. Delaware has attracted more than half of all public corporations and many private corporations in the U.S. (Delaware derives a third of its state revenue from the franchise tax!) Furthermore, Delaware is also the model followed by many other states. As a result, I see no point in teaching you other states' law. I occasionally use other countries' laws to expose you to alternative arrangements; the variance between countries is much larger than between U.S. states.

For similar reasons, I teach only corporations proper. I do not cover partnerships, limited liability companies (LLCs), or the many other entity forms now available.

These other forms are undoubtedly important in practice. But an introductory course cannot teach the nuanced differences between these forms, many of which lie in tax law. So I only give you a brief warning about involuntary partnership in the first class. However, the commonalities between the various entity forms are great. So if you understand corporate law and the underlying business problems, I trust you will easily learn the other forms when the need arises.

I am very grateful to Molly Eskridge, Scott Hirst, Zoe Piel, and Mengjie Zou for their amazing help in putting this together, and to Jordi Weinstock for the wonderful cover. —HS

Glossary

Bylaws = a corporation's secondary governing document (cf. DGCL 109(b)). The charter can provide, and usually does provide, that the board can amend the bylaws without shareholder consent (DGCL 109(a); contrast the charter itself, which can only be amended by board and shareholders jointly, DGCL 242(b)).

Certificate of incorporation = a corporation's founding and primary governing document (cf. DGCL 102).

Charter = certificate of incorporation.

Common stock / share = see share.

Debt holders = creditors.

DGCL = Delaware General Corporation Law, i.e., the basic Delaware statute. As a guide to this important statute, I have created the simplified DGCL.

Dividends = an official distribution of cash or other assets to all shareholders of one class. Even though dividends are generally the only way shareholders as a group get a return on their investment (individual shareholders can also sell their shares, but that only puts the buyer of the shares into the seller's shoes), dividends are in the board's discretion (DGCL 170(a)).

Equity; equity capital = the excess of assets over liabilities, if any (or equivalently, non-debt financing).

Equity holders = shareholders. The term derives from the fact that roughly speaking, equity is available for distribution to shareholders.

Limited liability = no liability (of shareholders). The expression "limited" comes from the observation that shareholders stand to lose whatever they put into the corporation, as this is available to satisfy the corporations' creditors' claims. However, shareholders have no liability beyond that, absent pathological circumstances.

Merger = the fusion of two corporations into one (cf. DGCL 251).

Preferred stock / share = stock with special rights ("preferences"), generally with respect to dividends. A standard term is that preferred shares are entitled to a certain dividend per year, payable if and when a dividend will be paid to common stockholders. In return, preferred shares often do not carry voting rights.

Public corporation = a corporation whose stock is publicly traded, usually on a regulated stock exchange such as the New York Stock Exchange.

Share = an interest in the corporation with rights that are defined by the corporation's charter. Unlike debt, shares do not provide a right to fixed payouts. Rather, the board decides if and when shareholders will receive so-called dividends. The default rule is that each share provides one vote (cf. DGCL 212) and equal dividend rights; such shares are called "common shares" or "common stock."

Stock = a synonym or collective term for shares (as in "twenty shares of the corporation's stock").

Part I: Introduction

Chapter 1. Foundations and Background

A. The Corporation

1. What is a corporation?

Formally speaking, a corporation is nothing but an **abstraction** to which we assign rights and duties. It exists independently of humans in the sense that it has indefinite life, and its assets and obligations are legally separate from those of any humans involved in its founding or administration. Today in the United States, anyone—a single individual, group, or another corporation or other entity—can create a corporation in a day for a couple hundred dollars in registration fees (e.g., using incorporate.com).

The corporate abstraction is an extraordinarily useful and widely used device for organizing relationships between various people and different assets. Most importantly, a group of people can pool their assets by transferring them to a corporation that will act as a single contracting interface with third parties (and with the owners among themselves, for that matter). Or a single person can set up multiple corporations to hold different assets and to enter into contracts relating to those assets. You can and should, therefore, also think of the corporation as a **contracting technology**. It facilitates contracting by partitioning and pooling assets.

Of course, being an abstraction rather than a real person, the corporation cannot exercise its rights, discharge its duties, or consume its profits by itself. Human beings must act on its behalf and ultimately consume its profits, if any. Humans can be involved directly, or through a chain of corporations (e.g., corporation A's sole shareholder is corporation B, whose shareholders are human beings). The basic **default governance** is simple: (common) shareholders elect the board of directors (cf. DGCL 211(b)), which formally manages the corporation (DGCL 141(a)), mostly by appointing the chief executive officer and other top management (cf. DGCL 142(a)), who in turn act on behalf of the corporation in day-to-day matters. As to consuming the profits, the board may decide to distribute available funds to shareholders—or not (cf. DGCL 170(a)). By default, each share confers one vote and the right to equal distributions per share (cf. DGCL 212(a) - the more shares you own, the more votes you have and the more of any distribution you get. Corporate law fills in the details: what if the board is unfaithful to shareholder interest? What if shareholders have divergent interests? Are there any other interests to be taken into account?

Technically, the corporation is not the only abstraction available for asset pooling and partitioning. There are variants such as the limited liability company (LLC) that have all or most of the features discussed here, and are subject to very similar rules. From the perspective of this introductory course, the differences are minor, and hence not covered.

2. What the corporation is not

The corporation is **not a person** like a human being. To be sure, we sometimes refer to corporations as "legal persons" (cf. 1 U.S.C. §1). But you should realize that this is just legalistic shorthand to emphasize the fact that a corporation can be the object and subject of legal claims. It does not mean that a corporation is a person in the sense that it has the same rights and obligations as human beings. Or have you ever heard of a corporation being drafted into military service? Or invoking a human right not to be tortured? As Chief Justice Roberts quipped in an opinion denying that AT&T could suffer "an unwarranted invasion of personal privacy" (*FCC v. AT&T*, 131 S.Ct. 1177, 1185 (2011)): "We trust that AT&T will not take it personally."

The corporation is also **not the same as a business**. A corporation may "own" a business, but they are not the same thing. A business is a collection of assets and a set of real world activities. A corporation is an abstract legal reference point to which we assign those assets. (Another formal note: In most jurisdictions, one technically cannot own a "business." Rather, one owns the assets that form the business, which include not only chattel and real property but also contracts, intellectual property, etc.)

3. Example 1: Mike's Pizza

To make this more concrete, think of your local pizza store. Perhaps it is called "Mike's Pizza," and Mike indeed runs the place. You might think that Mike is the "owner" of the store. In all likelihood, however, the formal "owner" of the pizza place — or rather the contracting party on the relevant contracts — is actually a corporation. The corporation might be called "Mike's Pizza Place Inc.," or "XYZ Corp." for that matter. XYZ Corp. might be (a) the lessee under any lease contract for the store building or other leased items, (b) the employer of any employees, (c) the owner of any real estate or chattel such as the pizza oven or the store sign, and (d) the contracting party with the payment system operator (so your payment for the pizza might show up under "XYZ Corp." on your credit card statement).

Of course, Mike might be XYZ Corp.'s sole shareholder, director, and chief executive officer (CEO). As shareholder, Mike would elect the board (here a single director), which in turn appoints the CEO. As CEO and director, Mike would then have plenary power to administer the business. And as shareholder, he might receive any profits as dividend. For many practical purposes, it is thus irrelevant if Mike owns the store outright or through a corporation. So what's the point of incorporating?

One benefit of incorporating can be convenience in contracting in certain transactions. If Mike ever wanted to sell the pizza place after incorporating, he would just sell the corporation — a single asset (or to be more precise, all his shares in the corporation, still just one collection of a uniform asset). By contrast, as a single owner, he would have to transfer all the assets individually.

Another convenience is that incorporating changes the default rule from unlimited liability to **limited liability**. The default rule for corporations is that shareholders, directors, and corporate officers are not liable for corporate debts (but they do stand to lose any assets they invested in the corporation as shareholders: hence the expression "limited liability" rather than "no liability"). By contrast, the default rule for single owners is the same as that for any other individual debt: full liability except for protection under the bankruptcy code. It is extremely important that you realize these are only default rules. Contracts can and often do transform limited liability into unlimited liability and vice versa. For example, a no-recourse mortgage contractually limits the borrower's liability to the value of the underlying real estate. Most importantly for present purposes, controlling shareholders such as Mike often contractually guarantee particular corporate debts such as bank loans (i.e., they contractually promise to pay the corporate debt if the corporation does not). In contractual relationships, the legal concept of "limited liability" is thus neither necessary nor sufficient to provide actual limited liability for shareholders; it merely facilitates it. The situation is different (and controversial) for most tort liability, as most tort creditors never consented, even implicitly, to the limited liability arrangement.

Questions

1. Do you, as a customer of Mike's Pizza, consent to Mike's limited liability?
2. Does it matter, legally or as a policy matter?
3. What if Mike himself negligently dropped a piece of glass onto your pizza — is he still protected by limited liability?
4. Should he be?

Another benefit is **entity shielding**. Entity shielding refers to a liability barrier in the opposite direction: Mike's personal creditors cannot demand payment or seize any assets from XYZ Corp. The personal creditors can only seize Mike's shares in XYZ Corp. Entity shielding is extremely useful because it allows those interacting with XYZ Corp. to focus their attention on the pizza store's assets and financial prospects, and not worry about Mike's other businesses. Imagine for example that Mike also runs a construction business in a different city. Without entity shielding, creditors from the construction business might seize assets of the pizza store, and vice versa. As a consequence, the two businesses' financial health could not be assessed independently of each other. By contrast, with entity shielding, a bank making a loan to develop the pizza store need only assess the financial prospects of the pizza store, i.e., XYZ Corp. And if the construction business does fail, XYZ Corp. can nevertheless continue business as usual. Entity shielding is more than a mere convenience in that it cannot be accomplished by contracting in the technical sense of the term (i.e., as opposed to the broader set of voluntary arrangements discussed below, which include corporate charters). That being said, the law also provides entity shielding to other entities such as partnerships.

One can neatly summarize limited liability and entity shielding with the simple legal construction of the corporation as a separate "legal person." "Naturally," one might say, separate persons are not liable for each other's debts. Importantly, however, the legal construction is only a convenient summary of policy choices that must be grounded elsewhere. For there is nothing natural about declaring the corporation a separate legal person in the first place (nor, for that matter, would there be anything natural about the opposite arrangement, in particular holding investors liable for all debts of the business). It is a convenient fiction, and the law does not adhere to it strictly. We will encounter exceptions in corporate law (notably "piercing the veil"), and there are many more in tax, antitrust, etc. See generally Felix Cohen, *Transcendental Nonsense and the Functional Approach*, 35 COLUM. L. REV. 809 (1935).

4. Example 2: Apple Inc.

I have just argued that the corporation can be useful for small, single-owner-manager businesses such as Mike's Pizza. But the corporation's full advantages only come into play in larger businesses with multiple shareholder-investors, many or most of whom have no direct involvement in management – i.e., there is **separation of ownership and control**. Almost all large firms are organized as corporations. And the majority of economic activity is bundled in large firms.

Think of Apple Inc. When its legendary co-founder and CEO Steve Jobs died, from a legal perspective all that happened was that the board of Apple Inc. had to appoint a new CEO. By contrast, if Steve Jobs had been the single owner of Apple, the entire business would have been part of his estate, presumably with deleterious consequences. Similarly, if the board of Apple Inc. decides to replace the CEO, it does so by simple resolution — it does not need to expropriate the old CEO.

Even more important than independence from its managers, Apple is independent from its shareholders, and the shareholders are excluded from management. Think of Apple Inc.'s millions of shareholders. Imagine the mayhem if any one of them could demand participation in Apple's management, or liquidation and distribution of Apple's assets. Or if the creditors of any one shareholder could demand payment from Apple, even just for a limited amount, and seize Apple's assets to the extent the payment is not forthcoming. And of course it would be impossible for Apple to enter into a contract or file a suit if this required the signatures of all its shareholders, just as no plaintiff could sue "Apple" if it required naming every single shareholder as a defendant. In other words, Apple Inc. as we know it could not exist without the convenience of a single fictitious "legal person," restricting shareholder involvement in management, and entity shielding.

Many think that Apple Inc. and other large corporations also could not exist without limited liability. The argument is that shareholder liability would deter wealthy investors (who are the ones most likely to be sued), would make the corporation's credit-worthiness dependent on its fluctuating shareholder base, and would interfere with diversification (the strategy to invest in many different assets so as to not put all eggs into one basket). There is reason to doubt this common wisdom, however. Limited liability distorts shareholders' incentives because they (fully) benefit from the upside but do not (fully) bear the downside of risky investments. And the problems of unlimited shareholder liability may be minor if liability is proportional to the number of shares held. Empirically, California provided for proportional shareholder liability until 1931, and American Express was organized with unlimited shareholder liability until 1965. It appears that shareholders largely viewed the shift to limited liability with indifference both in California and in American Express.

Back to indefinite life, and the inability of individual shareholders to demand liquidation. If an Apple shareholder wants to cash out, he or she can simply sell the shares. The default rule is that **shares are freely transferable**. This default rule complements indefinite life. It reconciles the corporation's need for continuity with individual shareholders' need for liquidity, i.e., the ability to convert their investment to cash. In smaller corporations, particularly family firms, however, the charter or shareholder agreements sometimes restrict transferability of shares. And even if sale is not restricted, there is often no market for a small corporation's shares at a price that fully reflects the corporation's value. In these cases, liquidity can be a major source of disagreement between shareholders.

In general, multi-member organizations also have governance problems that Mike's Pizza does not have. (I write "organizations" because the problems are not specific to corporations.) When the only shareholder (Mike) is also the only director, the only manager, and the only employee, there are no conflicts to resolve. But when there are millions of shareholders or more generally investors, a multi-member board, dozens of managers, and thousands of employees, conflicts abound. Millions are not necessary for conflicts to arise, however. The conflicts can be even more acrimonious when there are only two shareholders. Mitigating these conflicts is the main preoccupation of corporate law and of this course.

5. The broader picture

Before embarking on our study of conflict mitigation, here are a couple more basic facts to round out the corporate picture.

(a) Holdings and subsidiaries

Large businesses are usually not one but many corporations. Usually, a so-called "holding company" sits at the top of a pyramid of several layers of fully-owned subsidiary corporations. That is, the holding company owns 100% of the shares of several direct subsidiaries. These direct subsidiaries in turn own 100% of the shares of some other, indirect subsidiaries. And so on. This is a further illustration of the point that a corporation and a business are not the same thing.

Some advantages of the subsidiary structure are similar to the advantages of incorporating Mike's Pizza. Others include tax considerations and regulatory requirements. For example, Apple Inc. has become infamous for its use of Irish subsidiaries to "manage" its corporate tax liability. And yet, the relevant part of its corporate structure (see https://goo.gl/5w8qJQ at 20) appears simple compared to the full network of subsidiaries of, e.g., JP Morgan (https://goo.gl/sxx1FU), which comprises hundreds of subsidiaries.

In this course, we usually focus on the top level holding company because that is where the governance problems arise.

(b) Partnerships and other entity types

You may wonder what would happen if a multi-person firm did *not* incorporate. The answer is that "the association of two or more persons to carry on as co-owners a business for profit forms a partnership, whether or not the persons intend to form a partnership," unless the association was specifically formed under a separate statute such as the DGCL (which will generally require at least a registration). See section 202 of the Uniform Partnership Act of 1997; cf. section 6(1) of the Uniform Partnership Act of 1914.

This is a very dangerous default rule. Absent agreement to the contrary, (1) all partners have unlimited liability for partnership debt, (2) all partners have equal rights to participate in management, (3) any partner may be able to demand dissolution at any time, and (4) partnership interests are not transferable. It is a recipe for disaster.

You might now wonder how businesses could even operate before incorporation became generally available in the 19th century. There are three answers: First, some were lucky or corrupt enough to procure a special corporate charter from the queen/king or legislature (by "special act" or "private law"). Second, some businesses may indeed not have commenced or grown beyond a certain point because the corporate form was not available. Third, and most importantly, the partnership rules described above are merely the default rules. They can and usually are heavily tailored in the partnership agreement, provided that the partners are aware that they are forming a partnership.

For example, the partnership agreements of contemporary law firm partnerships reserve management to a committee, and provide for a regulated cash-out without dissolution if a partner wants to exit the partnership. The one thing that the partnership agreement cannot exclude in a traditional partnership is unlimited liability. To limit liability in a practical way, the law firm must choose a different entity type, as most large firms have done by now. In the past, before incorporation became freely available in England in the middle of the 19th century, English solicitors tailored trusts to approximate a corporation with limited liability.

(c) Contractual freedom

There is a more general theme here. Almost everything in U.S. corporate law can be modified by contract, at least if we understand contract in a broader sense to include charters and bylaws. For example, the charter can create separate classes of stock with different voting and distribution rights (DGCL 151(a), 212(a)). Even if a rule is mandatory on its face, like unlimited liability for partners in general partnerships, one can usually circumvent it by choosing an economically equivalent but legally different transaction or entity type, such as the limited liability partnership (LLP). See generally Bernard Black, *Is Corporate Law Trivial?*, 84 Nw. U. L. Rev. 542 (1990).

We will discuss the normative sense or nonsense of this state of affairs towards the end of the course. Until then, it is important to keep in mind that any judicial or legislative decision we read is contingent on the particular contractual arrangements chosen by the individuals involved. More to the point, as a budding corporate lawyer, you should always be thinking: what clause or arrangement could have avoided this problem?

Questions

1. Some large law firms choose to remain general partnerships. Can you guess why? (Do you know an example of a firm that's a general partnership?)
2. Which of the elements of the corporation could not have been provided by a simple contract between the participants (shareholders, managers, etc.)? In other words, if there were no corporate, partnership, or other organizational law but merely contract law, what would be missing?

B. Pizza Shop Exercise

Here is a little problem to warm up and introduce some basics of agency and partnership. Before attempting the problem, please read (!): Uniform Partnership Act (1914) §§ 6(1), 7(4), 9(1), 13, 15, 21(1), 29, 31(1)(b), 37, 38(1); Restatement of the Law (Third) Agency §§ 1.01, 1.04(7), 2.01, 2.03, 2.05, 3.01, 3.03, 4.01(1), 4.02(1), 6.01, 7.03, 8.01-03.

1. Litigator's perspective

Louis comes to you in distress. He tells you the following:

> Kathryn and I have been operating a pizza shop here in Cambridge for years. From a business perspective, we are doing extremely well. Personally, however, things have not been going so well lately. We have been fighting a lot. Today, I received a letter from Kathryn's attorney 'demanding and declaring that the business be dissolved and all assets liquidated to pay off the debt.' I have no idea what that means but I guess it's serious?

'All assets' is a fancy term, too! It is essentially one big pizza oven that we bought a year ago. We lease the store and our three delivery cars. We just renewed the leases a year ago for a five-year term. They all include penalties for early resolution, and they are not assignable. I reckon the penalties would collectively amount to $50,000 if we had to terminate the contracts now! And that oven, there's a problem there if we have to sell it now, too: it was custom-fit to our location, so I doubt we'd get more than $50,000 for it. But we still have that bank loan for about $100,000 that we used to finance it.

Is that all? Well, actually, there is another issue that came up right after I received the letter. That guy Steve – he generally buys our veggies and stuff. Goes to the wholesalers every week, they know he works for us. He gets the stuff, they debit our account, and we pay them by check later. Of course, after I got the letter, I told him not to buy anything today – who knows if we'll ever need it! But he just goes off and buys everything – and then crashes the car on the way back! Apparently he did major damage because now I am getting all these phone calls from various people and their attorneys demanding that I pay some crazy amounts. But I didn't drive that car, or put in those orders. Why should I pay for them?

And I sure hope I can keep the shop running. At least I don't want to be settled with that bank loan if we do have to close.

Questions

1. What do you think? Is there anything else you need to know?

2. Transactional View

We just looked at Louis and Kathy's pizza shop from a litigator's perspective. Most of the work of corporate lawyers, however, is to avoid disputes arising in the first place, in particular to design procedures that will resolve conflicts without litigation. So let's travel back in time six years.

Kathy and Louis ask you to set up the legal side of a pizza shop they envision. Louis has been working as a baker in a local bakery for many years. He will give up his job to become the pizza shop's general manager and, for the time being, only full-time employee. Kathy runs a marketing agency that does lots of business with mostly upscale restaurants. She will work on generating demand for the pizza shop in her spare time, while continuing to run her agency.

Kathy and Louis are childhood friends. They still spend a lot of time together. The idea for the pizza shop started at a recent dinner where they were both unhappy with the pizza. They concluded that they could do this better, and that there would be demand for better pizza in Cambridge. Over the next couple weeks, they worked out a business plan. They believe the pizza shop will be quite profitable.

They initially thought that Louis should set up the shop by himself, and that Kathy would just help out with the initial marketing. The problem is, however, that Louis doesn't have the cash to make the required investments. To be more exact, Louis is totally broke. A bank is willing to lend $100,000 to buy the pizza oven (the single biggest expense), taking a security interest in the oven. But the bank is not willing to lend unsecured for the initial operating expenses (supplies, drivers' salaries, etc.). Kathy and Louis are confident that the store will be profitable eventually. But they reckon it will take a couple months to get there. In the meantime, expenses will need to be paid, including Louis's living expenses.

As a solution, Kathy offers to invest some of her retirement savings in the pizza shop. The number they envision – roughly their estimate of six months of expenses – is $60,000. She and Louis also hope that Kathy may eventually join the business full time if things go well – in the long run, they dream of developing a chain.

Questions

1. Can you ethically represent both Kathy and Louis in this matter?

2. How would you advise Kathy and Louis to structure their business relationship? What eventualities should they prepare for? To make this more concrete, assume the only reasonable entity choice is a corporation (in reality, they might use an LLC). Which, if any, provisions would you advise they write into the charter or into the bylaws?

Read: Apple charter (Appendix 1); DGCL 102(b)(1), 109, 141(a)/(b), 212, 216, 242, and 275(a)/(b) (for present purposes, it is sufficient to read the simplified versions at simplifiedcodes.com)

Skim: Apple bylaws (Appendix 2).

Optional: take a glance at DGCL 273 (joint venture dissolution) and 341 et seq. (close corporations).

C. The Really Big Picture – and Basic Corporate Finance

Note: This section matters as much for terminology as for substance. If you have no background in business and finance, you should read it extremely carefully and look up any terms that you do not understand after reading twice.

As already mentioned above, the corporation is the vehicle of choice for pooling the resources of many investors. Before studying this vehicle in detail, it is worth zooming out for a moment to appreciate why these details matter—a lot!

1. The basic corporate investment relationship

The corporation is at the center of an elaborate system that matches cash-rich investors to cash-poor firms, and thereby enables life as we know it. On one side are **savers** who invest. For the time being, you can think of such savers as yourself when you start saving for retirement, usually through a tax-deferred plan like a 401(k). Savers invest first and foremost to **transfer value through time**, from today to the future: you put money into your 401(k) today and get it out when you retire in 40 years or so. On the other side are **firms** (or, in the beginning, a simple entrepreneur). Firms also wish to transfer value through time, but in the opposite direction, i.e., from the future to today: the firm expects to generate lots of cash in the future and offers to share it in return for financing today, without which it would not be able to generate the future cash in the first place ("Have idea, need money!").

To be sure, individual savers and entrepreneurs could decide to go it alone and put only their own money into a small-scale self-financed business. But in most industries, the investment required for efficient production far exceeds the wealth of individuals and thus requires **pooling resources**. For example, Apple has in excess of $300 billion in assets, financed by countless investors. Even if an individual could afford to finance an entire firm, it is generally preferable to spread the individual's wealth over many firms so as not to put all eggs into one basket, i.e., to reduce risk through **diversification**.

The importance of large-scale matching of savers and firms cannot be overstated. Without it, life as we know it would be impossible. There would be no personal computers, no smart phones, no cars (electric or not), and no electric skateboards. Nor should we take this matching for granted. In the U.S. and some other developed economies, the system matches savers and firms without much friction (cost): many firms can finance themselves on a grand scale at reasonable rates, and a great number of savers can expect returns not much below the rates paid by the firms. Elsewhere in the world, the spread between what savers get and what firms must pay is large, firms often find it hard to impossible to obtain funding at all, and saving is a treacherous affair. Given the enormous temptations for the recipients of financing not to pay it back, it is easy to see why the system might not work ("Tens of trillions of dollars entrusted to money-driven, focused people by naïve and absent-minded savers – what could go wrong?"). The astonishing thing is that it works so well in some parts of the world – and corporate law has a large part in that.

(a) Investors, intermediaries, and the lifecycle of firms

In fact, the system achieves nothing short of a miracle once you consider that the typical retirement plan saver invests the money for decades and never looks closely at what firms do with the money or even which firms have the money (more on this below). Firms, on the other hand, come and go and mutate all the time, as new ideas are born and old ones adapt or disappear. Throughout this lifecycle of firms, investors have to make important decisions or risk wasting their money on bad firms or being taken to the cleaners by the firms' managers or other investors. Fortunately, most of these decisions are made by professional investment managers—intermediaries—to whom the ultimate investors like us have entrusted their savings, relying on a well-functioning legal system and other institutions to ensure that we will eventually get our money back, and more.

A thumbnail sketch of a firm's lifecycle might be: In the beginning, an entrepreneur solicits financing from so-called **venture capital funds (VCs)** that specialize in early-stage financing. 90% of early stage companies fail. The VCs make their money off of the 10% that do not and reach the next stage: a "trade sale" to another company, or an **initial public offering (IPO)** of the corporation's stock to investors at large by means of registration with the S.E.C. and listing on a stock exchange. Depending on how the business develops, the corporation might later offer more stock to the public in a so-called **secondary equity offering (SEO)**, be acquired by another company, acquire other companies, or go bankrupt – or all of the above in various permutations.♦ Along the way, the corporation holds numerous shareholder votes and investor calls, engages in all sorts of financing transactions, and, last but decidedly not least, runs its business. This happens at tens of thousands of firms. Meanwhile, all that the ultimate investors are doing is to put their money into a bank account, annuity contract, retirement plan, etc., wait a couple decades, and leave the rest to financial intermediaries.

Such intermediaries include **banks and insurance companies**. Banks use funds received as deposits or savings to make loans. Insurance companies offer annuity products by taking savers' premia and investing them in firms; they also invest premia received from other insurance clients. Prudential regulation generally prohibits banks and insurance companies from investing in stocks, however, and thus they will feature less prominently in this course.

Retail investors' main way to invest in stocks and bonds (= tradeable debt) is through **mutual funds**. As the name suggests, mutual funds pool individual investor' funds and invest them in a pre-specified type of assets (e.g., S&P 500 stocks); each individual investor owns a share of the fund. By size, mutual funds are the big dog among intermediaries, especially in stocks: as of 2017, U.S. mutual funds had almost 20 trillion U.S. dollars under management. However, mutual funds are not the most active participants in corporate governance, nor are they present in all types of firms. This is largely because, in the name of investor protection, the Investment Company Act and the Investment Advisers Act, respectively, impose considerable restrictions on mutual funds and their management companies (like Fidelity or Vanguard). In particular, mutual funds must offer daily redemption at the fund's then-current net asset value (NAV), which makes it difficult to impossible for mutual funds to invest in illiquid assets, i.e., assets that do not trade in thick markets and hence cannot be sold quickly except at a major discount. Mutual funds therefore mostly invest in public securities, i.e., securities that are registered with the S.E.C. and, usually, admitted to trading on a trading venue such as a stock exchange. Moreover, mutual funds' diversification requirement and prohibition of performance fees makes it relatively unattractive for mutual fund managers to expend resources on effecting change at individual firms in the fund's portfolio.

Private funds—funds open only to select investors—are not subject to these restrictions and are thus present in all asset classes. They provide high-powered incentives to their managers for active management, and thus generate a disproportionate amount of trading and engagement. One small but important group

♦ Note in this regard that bankruptcy usually means restructuring or sale rather than liquidation, and firms not only buy but also sell a/k/a "spin off" subsidiaries and other parts of their business. For example, United Airlines was founded as Boeing Air Transport by William Boeing in 1927, merged with his Boeing Airplane Company in 1929, and spun out as United Airlines in 1934; it filed for bankruptcy in 2002, emerged from bankruptcy in 2006, and merged with Continental Airlines in 2013.

of private funds are the aforementioned VCs. A larger group of private funds called **private equity (PE)** buys mature companies (usually using plenty of additional debt financing), holds and reshapes them for a couple years, and then resells them. Both VCs and private equity funds have investment horizons of at least several years up to a decade and require their own investors to commit their capital for similar periods. All other private funds go by the catch-all name **hedge funds**. Their investment strategies and horizons differ greatly. Of particular importance for this course, so-called **activist** hedge funds seek to profit from changing the way a public company conducts its business, having taken a sizeable equity stake in the company that will increase in value if the company improves. **Merger arbitrage** hedge funds specialize in buying the equity of corporations that have announced to merge.

Investors in private funds include institutional investors such as public and private pension funds (e.g., CalPERS), endowments (e.g., Harvard's), and sovereign wealth funds (e.g., Saudi Arabia's). (The teams managing institutional investors are themselves intermediaries for the ultimate beneficiaries, such as employees and retirees.) Other investors in private funds are wealthy individuals, particularly ultra wealthy individuals who often have their own wealth management teams ("family offices"). In this connection, it is worth pointing out that the "savers" that invest their money in firms are not the average Joe: in the U.S., the top 1% own one third of all equity in public firms, and the top 10% own four fifths (these numbers include indirect ownership through pension funds etc.).

(b) Capital structure and corporate governance

As hinted above, there are two broad categories of financial claims that investors acquire in firms, in return for their investment: debt and equity. **Debt** is an IOU—a fixed claim. It includes loans from banks and others, as well as publicly traded debt securities called *bonds*. These payment claims can be enforced in court: creditors can sue for payment, and seize the corporation's assets if payment is not forthcoming. **Equity** (a/k/a shares, stock), on the other hand, provides no right to payment but usually provides voting rights to elect the corporation's board, which *may* determine to pay money to equity holders as a dividend or to buy back their stock.

If the corporation cannot pay its creditors—i.e., if it is *insolvent*—, unpaid creditors or the corporation itself may petition the bankruptcy court to open a **bankruptcy** procedure. Bankruptcy does not mean that the business of the corporation is liquidated. Rather, bankruptcy is a collective proceeding to settle various investors' claims, while preserving the business's going concern value, if any (potentially simply by selling the business, and then dividing the sale price between existing claimants).

The most important tool of bankruptcy law is its *automatic stay* of individual proceedings, which prevents inefficient liquidation by individual creditors racing to grab the corporation's assets and explains the expression "filing for bankruptcy *protection*." In bankruptcy, claimants are supposed to be paid in order of their seniority (see below). In particular, equity holders are supposed to get paid only after all creditors have been paid in full. Hence equity holders are often referred to as the corporation's *residual claimants*.

Debt and equity come in various flavors, including hybrids. This is especially true for debt. Not only do debt claims come in different maturities and with different ancillary rights, such as creditor undertakings to do or not to do something (**covenants**). Importantly, debt claims also differ in their **seniority**. Some creditors— so-called juniors—may contractually agree to subordination to certain other creditors—so-called seniors—in bankruptcy, i.e., to receive payment only after the latter have been paid in full. (Bankruptcy law itself also contains some seniority rules for special groups of creditors.) The debtor may grant a **security interest** in particular assets (e.g., a mortgage) to so-called secured creditors, which enables the secured creditors to obtain satisfaction of their claim from the sale of the asset prior to any other creditors, provided certain formalities, usually including a filing, have been complied with. (Security interests are also called collateral.) The debt contract may provide that the debt is **convertible** into equity at the election of the creditor and/or the corporation. The debt may also be issued together with **options**—known as **warrants** when issued by the corporation—, i.e., rights to purchase stock of the corporation at a pre-specified price (cf. DGCL 157).

Equity tends to be less varied, and most corporations only have one class of common stock. Of late, however, many prominent tech corporations such as Google, Facebook, or Snap have gone public with two or more different classes of stock ("**dual class**") to preserve the founders' control: one high-voting class reserved to the founders, and one low- or even non-voting class for outside investors. Many corporations also issue so-called **preferred stock**, which tends to have no voting rights but a dividend preference, i.e., the right to receive some specified minimum amount of dividends before any dividends can be paid to common stockholders (cf. DGCL 151(c)/(d)). Anything goes under Delaware corporate law: DGCL 151(a)). Voting and other rights may even be extended to creditors (DGCL 221).

A very important point is that the so-called capital structure formed by the combination of different claims on the corporation is just that: a structure to raise capital and ultimately to divide the returns, if any. There is nothing essential or even permanent about any of the claims or the investors who hold them. The same investors often hold different parts of the capital structure, such as debt and equity, simultaneously or at different points in time. Investors may trade in an out of the corporations' claims at any time (at least if they are traded in a liquid market). The corporation frequently extinguishes some claims by paying or buying them back and creates others by selling them in return for new investment. For example, the corporation may borrow money to buy back stock ("leveraged recapitalization"), issue stock to pay off debt, repay one loan by taking on another ("refinancing"), or offer to exchange one type of stock for another. (However, sensibly enough, shares owned by the corporation itself—"treasury shares"—do not have voting rights etc., see DGCL 160(c).)

Does capital structure matter? It obviously matters for the pricing of individual claims, as investors only pay for what they get. But what the corporation gives to holders of one claim it cannot give to another, and in light of the previous paragraph, the value of individual claims is hardly of deep interest (except, of course, to those buying or holding those claims!). The real question is whether the total value of all claims that the corporation can sell, and hence the total amount of financing it can raise, depends on the way the claims are delineated by contract, charter, and law? Specifically, does it matter which part of the dollars taken in by the firm (cash flows) go to which investors under which circumstances (**cash flow rights**), and what rights do those investors have to influence the decisions taken by the firm (**control rights**)?

Modigliani and Miller's famous benchmark result in corporate finance is that *if* the firm's cash flows were fixed and some other conditions held, it would not matter what sort of financial claims the firm issued – the total value of the claims would always be the same. As Miller once explained this proposition, it does not matter how you slice a pizza – it will always be the same amount of pizza. A corporation, however, is not a pizza: its cash flows depend crucially on how it is managed, which in turn depends on how it is governed, i.e., who has which control rights and how they exercise them. Cash flow rights provide incentives to exercise control rights in a certain manner. These incentives can be more or less aligned with increasing the value of the pie (or size of the pizza, if you will). The division and bundling of cash flow and control rights thus matters a great deal.

Corporate and bankruptcy law have some role in the division and bundling of rights, but most of it is done by contract writ large, including the corporate charter. This is inevitable because businesses differ and hence need different governance terms adjusted to the business. In particular, businesses differ in the amount of debt they can service. Debt offers important advantages. First, it is tax advantaged: interest is tax deductible, while dividends are not. Second, debt is less information-sensitive: creditors only need to assess the corporation's ability to repay the loan rather than the corporation's full potential. Last but not least, creditors' return expectations are backed up by a hard legal claim and its threat of judicial enforcement and bankruptcy, whereas shareholders are at the mercy of the board. This last feature, however, also makes debt inflexible: it will lead to costly litigation, bankruptcy, or even liquidation whenever the actual cash flows fall short of projected cash flows, or at least give creditors the ability to extract concessions in renegotiating the debt. That is why only stable businesses with predictable cash flows tend to use a lot of debt, while more volatile businesses, particularly startups, rely mostly or exclusively on equity financing. Most of this course will be concerned with the ways in which corporate law seeks to ensure that shareholders will get a return even though they lack a hard claim to repayment.

A final note on capital structure and corporate governance is that every possible arrangement is a compromise, and perfection is impossible. Ex ante, every participant in the business would agree that the goal is to maximize the size of the total pie (or pizza, if you prefer) because that will enable everyone to get a bigger slice (the division can be adjusted by side payments). Once the business gets under way, however, whoever has control over a decision will be tempted to use that control to get a bigger slice, even if doing so reduces the size of the total pie. For example, managers may favor growing the business beyond the efficient size if they enjoy the greater power and prestige that comes from running a bigger firm. Creditors may favor inefficient liquidation if continuation, while profitable in expectation, is also risky, such that creditors stand to lose but not much to gain from continuation (remember that creditors' claims are fixed!). Inversely, shareholders may favor inefficient continuation if continuation, while unprofitable in expectation, presents at least the possibility of a positive outcome whereas the liquidation proceeds would go fully or mostly to creditors. The point is that as soon as people pool resources, conflicts of interest are unavoidable. The goal is to mitigate such conflicts; they cannot be eliminated.

(c) Valuation

> *Note:* This subsection is conceptually denser and more algebraic than anything else in this course. You may find it challenging on first reading.

Above, I said tongue-in-cheek that the value of individual claims does not matter in the big scheme of things. Of course, to individual investors, the value of their claim is all that matters. And because of that, understanding how different actions affect the value of individual claims is crucial to understand the incentives of those holding those claims.

To value a claim, one usually starts with the claim's **expected future cash flows**. Expected cash flows are the probability-weighted average of the cash flows that the investor will receive in all the conceivable scenarios. For example, if the investment will return either $2 million or nothing with equal probability, the expected cash flows are 50% × $2 million + 50% × 0 = $1 million. In the real world, estimating expected cash flows requires understanding the business and the capital structure, particularly—for debt—the seniority structure and security interests. Usually, such estimates are fraught with very considerable uncertainty, especially for equity (cf. discussion of information-sensitivity above).

The next step is to **discount** the future cash flows **to present value** for the time value of money and a risk premium, to name only the most important ones. The **time value of money** arises from the simple fact that in the world we live in, all investors have the alternative to put their money into other investments that are expected to pay back the same amount of money *plus a positive return* in the future. In particular, investors have the alternative to invest in U.S. government bonds that will pay back the same amount of money plus interest with certainty.[1] Thus, to persuade investors to give their money to the corporation, the corporation has to offer more than the interest paid by the government. How much more? That depends on the risk of the corporation's claim. Risk in this context does not mean the probability of non-payment per se: that is already accounted for in the calculation of *expected* future cash flows. Rather, risk here means the variance or volatility of the expected cash flows. For example, for their retirement, most people would rather have $1 million for sure rather than a 50/50 chance of $2 million or nothing (note that the expected cash flows are the same, namely 50% × $2 million + 50% × 0 = 100% × $1 million). That said, investors can diversify away most risk by investing small amounts in many different assets rather than everything in one asset. By and large, investors thus receive a **risk premium** only for **systematic risk**, i.e., risk that is undiversifiable because it is likely to hit all assets at the same time, such as a global recession. (Of course, individual investors would prefer to receive premia for all sorts of things, but in a competitive financial market, investors compete away most other premia – ultimately, the **expected return** on an investment is set by the supply and demand for capital.)

Let us consider an extremely stylized example. Imagine we knew for certain that a firm will be in operation for only one year, after which it will liquidate all its assets and

---

[1] Well, actually, the government bond also pays you a compensation for expected inflation. But we'll assume our business's outcomes are measured in nominal terms, so including an inflation premium is appropriate.

distribute them to its investors. Imagine further that we magically know that there are only three possible outcomes, all equally likely: after liquidation but before distribution, the firm will hold (1) $0, (2) $100, or (3) $200. What is this firm worth? Start with the expected future cash flows: $\frac{1}{3} \times \$0 + \frac{1}{3} \times \$100 + \frac{1}{3} \times \$200 = \$100$. To discount those future cash flows to present value, we need to know the time value of money and the firm-specific risk premium. As mentioned above, the time value of money is what you could earn on a government bond of the same duration.° Let's assume the government currently offers 1% on a one year bond. What is the right risk premium? It depends on the firm! The more the success of the firm is correlated with the health of the economy, the higher the risk premium. How high? It depends on what financial markets demand—or equivalently, what investors can get elsewhere—, which in practice we would estimate by looking at similar firms. Imagine we found the right premium to be 10%. In that case, our firm would be worth $\$100/(1+1\%+10\%)=\$90.09$.♦

♦ At the limit, if the success of the firm were purely idiosyncratic—e.g., it depends on whether or not a patent will be upheld in court—, then the appropriate risk premium would be zero, and our firm would be worth $\$100/(1+1\%+0\%)=\$99.01$.

Having valued the firm as a whole, let us value individual claims on it. Imagine the firm is organized as a corporation and only has two claimants: a creditor owed $100, and a shareholder.

Let us start with the creditor and observe that the creditor's claim is not necessarily worth $100—the corporation has promised $100, but whether it will pay that much is an entirely different question, and how to value those payments yet another.♦♦ Concretely, the corporation will not be able to pay anything to the creditor in case 1 where it ends up holding $0 (perhaps *the shareholder* would be able to pay, but, because of limited liability, the shareholder will not need to pay and presumably won't). In the other two cases 2 and 3, the corporation will be able to pay $100 but will not pay more than that (in case 3, it *could* pay more but it won't because the creditor only has a fixed claim for $100). Thus, the expected cash flows to the creditor are $\frac{1}{3} \times \$0 + \frac{1}{3} \times \$100 + \frac{1}{3} \times \$100 = \$66.67$. As to the appropriate discount rate, observe that the creditor's claim is less volatile than the firm as a whole: in two out of three states, the creditor gets the same amount of money. The appropriate risk premium will thus be lower than for the firm as a whole (which was 10%); assume it is 7%. The time value of money is still 1%. Thus, the creditor's claim is worth $\$66.67/(1+1\%+7\%)=\$61.73$.

♦♦ Nor did the creditor necessarily invest $100: $100 is merely the **face value** of the claim, i.e., the promised amount. In fact, given the time value of money, the investor presumably invested less than $100!

Meanwhile, the shareholder as residual claimant gets whatever is left over after paying the creditor, which is nothing in cases 1 and 2 and $100 in case 3, for an expected cash flow of $\frac{1}{3} \times \$0 + \frac{1}{3} \times \$0 + \frac{1}{3} \times \$100 = \$33.33$ (alternatively, we could have found this number by subtracting the creditor's expected cash flows from those of the corporation as a whole). The shareholder's claim is riskier than the firm as a whole because the shareholder will only be paid in the best possible case; let us assume the appropriate risk premium is 16.5%. Then, the shareholder's claim is worth $33.33/(1+1\%+16.5\%)=\$28.37.$[2]

For obvious reasons, the valuation approach exposited above is called **discounted cash-flow analysis (DCF)**. An alternative to DCF is to use **comparables**: one calculates some valuation ratio (or "multiple") for comparable claims, and then assumes that the same ratio will hold for the claim under examination. For example, to value the shares of company A (say, Pepsi), one might look at comparable company B (say, Coca-Cola), calculate the ratio of company B's stock price to B's current earnings per share (EPS; roughly, firm profits divided by number of shares outstanding), and then calculate company A's share value as A's EPS times B's share value divided by B's EPS, *on the assumption* that A and B should have the same price/EPS multiple. (Thus, if Coca-Cola's share is worth $150, Coca-Cola's EPS is $10 per share, and Pepsi's EPS is $8 per share, then Pepsi's share is worth $8 × $150/$10 = $120, as valued by EPS multiple.) The advantage of the comparables approach to valuation is that it avoids the difficult task of estimating company A's expected cash flows. The disadvantage is that one must not only assume that company B is already correctly valued, but also that both companies will develop in parallel from their current starting point. The latter assumption is never exactly true and even the approximation may be very bad. In practice, most valuations triangulate from a combination of DCF and multiple comparable firms.

Finally, knowing a claim's present value, or PV, is not enough to make an investment decision. At the risk of stating the obvious, the price of the claim also matters. The investment is appealing only if the *net* **present value (NPV)**, i.e., PV minus price, is positive.

---

[2] In this example, the value of the creditor's claim and the value of the shareholder's claim add up to the value of the firm as a whole. This might appear unsurprising because the two claims are the only claims on the firm, and value cannot evaporate or appear from out of nowhere. Notice, however, that the algebraic equivalence depended on the risk premia: it would not hold with different risk premia (e.g., a lower risk premium for equity). Modigliani and Miller, mentioned above, are famous for showing that, under certain conditions, risk premia must be such that the equivalence does hold. As also mentioned above, however, Modigliani-Miller is merely a benchmark result. In reality, risk premia may not obey the equivalence exactly. More importantly, Modigliani-Miller applies to fixed cash flows; if capital structure influences cash flows, then all bets are off. In the example above, an important omission was taxes: the mix of debt and equity generally influences tax burdens, and it would not even make sense to value "the firm" without taking into account its financing and associated expected taxes.

D. Securities Law Primer

State corporate law is very closely intertwined with federal securities law. The link is so close that it is worth giving you a very brief introduction of some elements that will come up again and again in this course. (In other countries, these elements might be included in "corporate law." The distinction is artificial.)

Securities are, roughly, tradable investments such as shares and bonds (tradable debt claims). For our purposes, the relevant statutes are the Securities Act of 1933, and the Securities Exchange Act of 1934 ("Exchange Act"). Both grant broad powers to the U.S. Securities and Exchange Commission (SEC). In particular, the SEC has promulgated very detailed rules implementing the securities laws.

The **Securities Act** is chiefly concerned with the initial disclosure upon a first sale of a security to the public in a so-called registration statement. We will therefore encounter it less often.

The **Exchange Act**, on the other hand, is ubiquitous. Among other things, it regulates ongoing corporate disclosure, and trading in corporate securities. Most provisions of the Exchange Act apply only to "registered securities," which include all securities that are publicly traded on a stock exchange or elsewhere. This excludes securities of private companies, i.e., companies whose securities are not marketed to the public, and in particular not traded on a stock exchange. Private companies include not only small firms but also some large ones like Uber (as of December 2017).

In terms of **disclosure**, the Exchange Act requires, inter alia, the following filings with the SEC, who makes them publicly available on **EDGAR:**

- **Annual** disclosure of the corporation's financial and business situation on **Form 10-K**. This disclosure is quite comprehensive. For example, corporations have to disclose audited financial statements and many details about their executive compensation arrangements.
- **Quarterly** disclosure on **Form 10-Q**. Less comprehensive than 10-K.
- **Ad hoc** disclosure of certain specified events such as a merger on **Form 8-K**.
- **Proxy statements**, i.e., comprehensive disclosure from anyone soliciting shareholder votes, including the corporation itself – see the shareholder voting part of the course.
- Anyone proposing certain important transactions must disclose background, terms, and plans – details when we get there.
- **Ownership interests** above 5% on **Schedule 13D**.

- **Trades by corporate insiders** (directors, officers, and anyone owning 10% or more of a corporation's stock) (Exchange Act §16(a)).

Since 2000, SEC **Regulation FD** (for "fair disclosure") additionally provides, in the SEC's own words, that "when an issuer discloses material nonpublic information to certain individuals or entities—generally, securities market professionals, such as stock analysts, or holders of the issuer's securities who may well trade on the basis of the information—the issuer must make public disclosure of that information."

The Securities Laws and the SEC's rules thereunder also provide private and public remedies for false or misleading statements. The most important provision is SEC **Rule 10b-5**, a broad anti-fraud rule implementing section 10(b) of the Exchange Act. Courts have implied a private right of action under this and similar rules, which sustain an industry of securities class action lawyers. We will deal with rule 10b-5 and others when we cover securities trading in Part IV: of the course.

E. Alphabet/Google Exercise

- Read the Wikipedia excerpts on Alphabet/Google below and look up any terms that you do not know (most were explained in the previous sections!).
- Find out who Alphabet's three major stockholders are, both in terms of (a) voting rights and (b) cash-flow rights.[*]
  - o What are their stakes worth, approximately, given Alphabet's current stock price?
  - o Beyond their names, who are they, i.e., what is their economic role? To the extent they are businesses, not individuals, what is their business model?
- As you know from the last question, voting rights and cash flow rights do not go hand in hand in Alphabet. In particular, Class A and Class B shares have equal cash flow rights but unequal voting rights. This is laid down in certain provisions of Alphabet's charter. Which ones? (You can find the Alphabet charter in the SEC database with a little effort, or with no effort on the Alphabet investor relations webpage.)
- Since 2014, Google/Alphabet's charter also authorizes Class C shares. What voting and cash flow rights do they have? Why do you think Google/Alphabet created this additional class?
- In 2006, Google bought YouTube for around $1.5 billion. Find out how Google paid the YouTube sellers. (It's ok to Google this one.)

1. Google: Excerpt from Wikipedia Entry[3]

Google is an American multinational technology company specializing in Internet-related services and products that include online advertising technologies, search, cloud computing, software, and hardware.

---

[*] There are two ways to find out who those major stockholders are. One possibility is to Google them. A more reliable method is to look up Alphabet's proxy statement in the SEC's public database. Go to SEC.gov, select Filings/Company_Filings_Search, search for Alphabet Inc. or its ticker GOOG, and then for its latest form DEF 14A (April 2018), which lists common stock ownership under that heading. One big advantage of this method is that it also works for much less famous public companies.

[3] Entry on "Google," accessed 1/16/2017, footnotes removed; reproduced under Creative Commons license CC-BY-SA (http://creativecommons.org/licenses/by-sa/3.0/).

Google was founded in 1996 by Larry Page and Sergey Brin while they were Ph.D. students at Stanford University, California. Together, they own about 14 percent of its shares and control 56 percent of the stockholder voting power through supervoting stock. They incorporated Google as a privately held company on September 4, 1998. An initial public offering (IPO) took place on August 19, 2004, and Google moved to its new headquarters in Mountain View, California, nicknamed the Googleplex.

In August 2015, Google announced plans to reorganize its various interests as a conglomerate called Alphabet. Google, Alphabet's leading subsidiary, will continue to be the umbrella company for Alphabet's Internet interests. Upon completion of the restructure, Sundar Pichai became CEO of Google, replacing Larry Page, who became CEO of Alphabet.

Rapid growth since incorporation has triggered a chain of products, acquisitions and partnerships beyond Google's core search engine (Google Search). It offers services designed for work and productivity (Google Docs, Sheets and Slides), email (Gmail/Inbox), scheduling and time management (Google Calendar), cloud storage (Google Drive), social networking (Google+), instant messaging and video chat (Google Allo/Duo/Hangouts), language translation (Google Translate), mapping and turn-by-turn navigation (Google Maps), video sharing (YouTube), taking notes (Google Keep), and organizing and editing photos (Google Photos). The company leads the development of the Android mobile operating system, the Google Chrome web browser and Chrome OS, a lightweight operating system based around the Chrome browser. Google has moved increasingly into hardware; from 2010 to 2015, it partnered with major electronics manufacturers in the production of its Nexus devices, and in October 2016, it launched multiple hardware products (the Google Pixel, Home, Wifi, and Daydream View), ...

An August 2011 report estimated that Google had almost one million servers in data centers around the world. It processed over one billion search requests per day in 2009, and about 20 petabytes of data each day in 2008.

Alexa, a company that monitors commercial web traffic, lists Google.com as the most visited website in the world. Several other Google services also figure in the top 100 most visited websites, including YouTube and Blogger. Google has been the second most valuable brand in the world for 4 consecutive years, and has a valuation in 2016 at $133 billion.

Google's mission statement from the outset was "to organize the world's information and make it universally accessible and useful," and its unofficial slogan was "Don't be evil". In October 2015, the motto was replaced in the Alphabet corporate code of conduct by the phrase: "Do the right thing". Google's commitment to such robust idealism has been increasingly called into doubt due to a number of actions and behaviours which appear to contradict this.

History

Google began in January 1996 as a research project by Larry Page and Sergey Brin when they were both PhD students at Stanford University in Stanford, California.

While conventional search engines ranked results by counting how many times the search terms appeared on the page, the two theorized about a better system that analyzed the relationships between websites. They called this new technology PageRank; it determined a website's relevance by the number of pages, and the importance of those pages, that linked back to the original site.

Page and Brin originally nicknamed their new search engine "BackRub", because the system checked backlinks to estimate the importance of a site. Eventually, they changed the name to Google, originating from a misspelling of the word "googol", the number one followed by one hundred zeros, which was picked to signify that the search engine was intended to provide large quantities of information. Originally, Google ran under Stanford University's website, with the domains google.stanford.edu and z.stanford.edu.

The domain name for Google was registered on September 15, 1997, and the company was incorporated on September 4, 1998. It was based in the garage of a friend (Susan Wojcicki) in Menlo Park, California. Craig Silverstein, a fellow PhD student at Stanford, was hired as the first employee.

Financing, 1998 and initial public offering, 2004

The first funding for Google was an August 1998 contribution of $100,000 from Andy Bechtolsheim, co-founder of Sun Microsystems, given before Google was incorporated. At least three other angel investors invested in 1998: Amazon.com founder Jeff Bezos, Stanford University computer science professor David Cheriton, and entrepreneur Ram Shriram. ...

After some additional, small investments through the end of 1998 to early 1999, a new, $25 million round of funding was announced on June 7, 1999, with major investors including the venture capital firms Kleiner Perkins Caufield & Byers and Sequoia Capital. ...

[Following the closing of the $25 million financing round, Sequoia encouraged Brin and Page to hire a CEO. Brin and Page ultimately acquiesced and hired Eric Schmidt as Google's first CEO in March 2001. In October 2003, while discussing a possible initial public offering of shares (IPO), Microsoft approached the company about a possible partnership or merger. The deal never materialized.][4]

Google's initial public offering (IPO) took place five years later on August 19, 2004. At that time Larry Page, Sergey Brin, and Eric Schmidt agreed to work together at Google for 20 years, until the year 2024.

At IPO, the company offered 19,605,052 shares at a price of $85 per share. Shares were sold in an online auction format using a system built by Morgan Stanley and Credit Suisse, underwriters for the deal. The sale of $1.67 bn (billion) gave Google a market capitalization of more than $23bn. By January 2014, its market capitalization[*] had grown to $397bn. ...

[*] Market cap(italization) = number of shares outstanding × price per share. By this measure, Alphabet/Google is currently the 3rd largest company in the world, with a market capitalization of $845 billion as of 8/16/2018.

There were concerns that Google's IPO would lead to changes in company culture. Reasons ranged from shareholder pressure for employee benefit reductions to the fact that many company executives would become instant paper millionaires. As a reply to this concern, co-founders Sergey Brin and Larry Page promised in a report to potential investors that the IPO would not change the company's culture. ...

The stock performed well after the IPO, with shares hitting $350 for the first time on October 31, 2007, primarily because of strong sales and earnings in the online advertising market. The surge in stock price was fueled mainly by individual investors, as opposed to large institutional investors and mutual funds. GOOG shares split into GOOG Class C shares and GOOGL class A shares. The company is listed on the NASDAQ stock exchange under the ticker symbols GOOGL and GOOG, and on the Frankfurt Stock Exchange under the ticker symbol GGQ1. These ticker symbols now refer to Alphabet Inc., Google's holding company, since the fourth quarter of 2015.

---

[4] This insert is from the separate Wikipedia entry on "History of Google." For copyright, see previous note.

Part II: The Basics

Chapter 2. The Basic Corporate Law Problem

This part of the course will acquaint you with the basics of U.S. corporate law. It will also give you an idea of what boards actually do, and introduce you to a variety of shareholder types and relationships.

A. The Basic Problem

The basic corporate governance problem is how to control those who have been entrusted with the assets assembled in the corporation: managers and directors.

This economic problem is called an *"agency problem"*: how to ensure that the "agents" (managers/directors) act in furtherance of the "principals'" (shareholders') interests rather than the agents' own interest? If this agency problem cannot be addressed satisfactorily, investors will not be willing to put their money into corporations, and the wealth generating machine matching savers and businesses to finance investment won't work (see The Really Big Picture above). Not employing agents at all is not a solution because centralized management is essential in large organizations. Instead, the trick is to devise appropriate controls.

(NB: the economic terminology of "agent" and "principal" employed in this section is related to, but much broader than, the legal terminology in the law of agency. Legally, managers are agents for the corporation, not for shareholders, and directors aren't legal agents for anybody – in particular, they are not subject to shareholder directives. From an economic perspective, however, the corporation is a fiction — a convenient way of describing relationships between human beings. In this perspective, directors and managers ultimately work for shareholders and hence are shareholders' agents in an economic, though not legal, sense.)

B. The Basic Partial Solutions

1. Shareholder voting and fiduciary duties

U.S. corporate law offers two basic solutions to the corporate agency problem: shareholder voting, and fiduciary duties enforced by shareholder lawsuits.

First, shareholders vote on certain important corporate decisions. In particular, shareholders elect, and can remove, directors, who in turn appoint management. This is often referred to as "corporate democracy" but, as we will see shortly, shareholder voting differs considerably from political elections.

Second, directors and managers hold their corporate powers as fiduciaries, i.e., for the sole benefit of "the corporation and its shareholders." As fiduciaries, directors and managers owe a duty of care and a duty of loyalty to "the corporation and its shareholders." Crucially, U.S. courts liberally grant shareholders standing to enforce these duties in court through derivative suits:

> The derivative action developed in equity to enable shareholders to sue in the corporation's name where those in control of the company refused to assert a claim belonging to it. The nature of the action is two-fold. First, it is the equivalent of a suit by the shareholders to compel the corporation to sue. Second, it is a suit by the corporation, asserted by the shareholders on its behalf, against those liable to it.

> —*Aronson v. Lewis*, 473 A.2d 805, 811 (Del. 1984).

2. Other shareholder rights

In addition to voting rights and standing to sue, shareholders also have the right to access certain corporate information. This is an important ancillary right because both shareholder voting and derivative suits require information to work well. DGCL 220 allows shareholders "to inspect for any proper purpose ... [t]he corporation's ... books and records." Furthermore, publicly traded corporations must make extensive affirmative disclosures under the securities laws.

Finally, shareholders can sell their stock. This is important for individual shareholders' liquidity, i.e., shareholders' ability to convert the value of their corporate investment into cash when necessary. However, this so-called Wall Street Walk is useless, at least by itself, as a protection against bad management. If the corporation has bad management, its value to shareholders will be less than it could be, and its stock price will be discounted to reflect this. So a shareholder can sell, but that just locks in the loss from bad management; it does not fix it. (By analogy, an arson victim's right to sell the land with the burnt ruins hardly compensates the victim for, nor prevents, the arson.) Selling is useful only in as much as it enables a *buyer* to amass a large enough position from which to challenge the sitting board using the first two tools (voting and suing).

3. Default rules vs. contractual arrangements

Importantly, U.S. corporate law generally sets only default rules. Charter provisions and other contractual or quasi-contractual arrangements can supplement or alter all or most of these rules. Indeed, "contractual" arrangements pervade corporate law, from the definition of shareholder rights and allocation of management power in the corporate charter, to bylaws on voting, to executive compensation contracts. Read: DGCL 102(b)(1), 151(a), 141(a), and 109(b).

C. Variations on the Basic Problem

1. The board as a monitor

So far, I have framed the basic problem of corporate governance as how to control managers *and* the board. An important tool of corporate governance, however, is control of managers *by* the board. Arguably, the primary role of a board composed mostly of outside members (i.e., non-management) is to select, monitor, and thus control managers. It is now standard or even legally required for public corporations' boards to consist mostly of independent directors, i.e., directors who do not have other relationships with the corporation, especially not a role in management. That being said, in U.S. corporations, it is still customary for CEOs and other top managers to sit on the board and even to chair it.

Some countries go even further and fully separate outside directors and management. Under the so-called two-tier system, a "supervisory board" composed exclusively of outside directors is superimposed on the "management board" composed of top managers. Shareholders elect the supervisory board, which in turn appoints and monitors the management board. (In some jurisdictions the supervisory board is self-nominating or partially elected by the corporation's employees.)

But while directors may indeed monitor management, this only shifts the basic problem one level up: how can we control those who have been entrusted with this monitoring role? *Quis custodiet ipsos custodes?* (Who monitors the monitors?)

2. Dominant shareholders

Monitoring the monitor is a particularly acute problem with respect to large, dominant shareholders. Most public corporations around the world have a dominant shareholder. In the U.S. and in the U.K., dispersed ownership is the norm but far from universal. On the positive side, dominant shareholders help overcome shareholders' collective action problem in monitoring managers and the board. On the flip side, however, dominant shareholders may attempt to extract a disproportionate share for themselves. Delaware limits such minority abuse by imposing fiduciary duties on "controlling shareholders." Other jurisdictions impose super-majority requirements, or outright prohibit certain transactions, etc.

In general, a shareholder needs to own close to 50% of the outstanding stock to **control** the corporation. ("close to" because some other shareholders tend not to vote, such that the controlling stockholder can command a majority of the stock *voted* at the meeting even though owning less than a majority of the stock *outstanding*.) However, if the corporation issues multiple classes of stock with differentiated voting rights ("dual class stock"), a shareholder can control (by owning the high-voting stock) even while owning only a small fraction of the cash flow rights (cf. Google Exercise above, and "Shareholder Democracy" below). This exacerbates the conflict of interest with the other shareholders: the lower the controlling shareholder's proportional economic stake in the corporation, the higher the controlling shareholder's gain from diverting value from the corporation into the controlling shareholder's own pockets (cf. Some (Not So) Fictitious Examples in the Duty of Loyalty section below).

Many non-U.S. jurisdictions prohibit dual class stock, but dominant shareholders employ a **pyramid** structure to achieve a very similar result. To wit, the dominant shareholder will be the majority shareholder of corporation A, which is in turn the majority shareholder of corporation B, which may be a majority shareholder of corporation C, and so on. In such a structure, the dominant shareholder controls each of the layers even though economically the dominant shareholder only receives much less than 50% of the cash flows from the lower layers. For example, if the dominant shareholder owns 50.01% of the stock of A, which owns 50.01% of B, which owns 50.01% of C, then the dominant shareholder indirectly controls C even though the dominant shareholder will receive only 50.01% × 50.01% × 50.01% = 12.51% of any dividend paid by C and passed through B and A to their respective shareholders. In the U.S., pyramids are tax-disadvantaged because each layer is subject to corporate income tax (such that multiplying layers means multiplying tax), and for this and perhaps other reasons virtually inexistent. (For the avoidance of doubt: U.S. corporations do employ holding structures where the top-level corporation owns several subsidiaries, which may own sub-subsidiaries and so on, but all the subsidiaries are wholly-owned by their respective parent(s), such that control and cash flow rights go hand in hand; the IRS exempts such wholly-owned structures from multiple taxation.)

3. Protecting other constituencies

I defer until the end of the book the question of whether corporate law does or should protect constituencies other than shareholders (often called "stakeholders"), such as creditors, workers, or customers. For the time being, I just note that the question is not whether stakeholders should be protected at all, but whether they should be protected by the tools of corporate law—that is, beyond the level of protection afforded by contract (loan agreements, employment contracts, collective bargaining, etc.), and by other branches of law (employment law, labor law, consumer law, etc.).

4. Enforcement

Enforcement and its problems are of paramount importance for corporate law. At the extreme, if general law enforcement were too weak, managers could, for example, simply abscond with the corporation's money. No fiduciary duties, shareholder litigation, or shareholder voting could protect against this. Fortunately, criminal law enforcement in the U.S. is strong enough that outright fraud and theft are not the most pressing concerns and can be mostly ignored in this course.

In the more subtle form of inadministrability, however, enforcement problems are key to understanding the rationale behind much of corporate law — and indeed behind much of law generally. Administrability refers to courts' ability to administer the laws as written. The problem is that courts often lack the requisite information. For this reason, many superficially appealing rules do not work as intended. For example, it is certainly desirable that managers always do only what is best for shareholders, or at least what they think is best for shareholders, and that they do so flawlessly or at least to the best of their abilities. Formally speaking, that is indeed more or less what fiduciary duties require of managers. That does not mean, however, that it is realistic to think that courts could actually enforce such a standard. Courts may not know what action was best for shareholders, much less what the managers truly thought was best for shareholders. Nor can courts easily know whether managers gave their best efforts or loyalty. Courts will inevitably misjudge many careful, loyal actions as disloyal or careless, and vice versa — even after costly and lengthy litigation.

Faced with such difficulties, it may be best to forego costly judicial review altogether unless a transaction raises a red flag. The reddest of red flags is when the decision would financially benefit the decision-makers or their affiliates more than (other) shareholders. That, in a nutshell, is the approach taken in Delaware and other U.S. states and epitomized by the **business judgment rule**. We will dive deep into the details later. For now, here is the scoop in the words of the seminal case, *Aronson v. Lewis*:

> The business judgment rule is an acknowledgment of the managerial prerogatives of Delaware directors under Section 141(a). It is a presumption that in making a business decision the directors of a corporation acted on an informed basis, in good faith and in the honest belief that the action taken was in the best interests of the company. Absent an abuse of discretion, that judgment will be respected by the courts. ...
>
> [However, the rule's] protections can only be claimed by disinterested directors . ... From the standpoint of interest, this means that directors can neither appear on both sides of a transaction nor expect to derive any personal financial benefit from it in the sense of self-dealing . ... See 8 Del.C. § 144(a)(1).
>
> [Moreover], to invoke the rule's protection directors have a duty to inform themselves, prior to making a business decision, of all material information reasonably available to them. Having become so informed, they must then act with requisite care in the discharge of their duties. While the Delaware cases use a variety of terms to describe the applicable standard of care, our analysis satisfies us that under the business judgment rule director liability is predicated upon concepts of gross negligence.
>
> —473 A.2d 805, 812 (Del. 1984) (footnotes and internal references omitted).

More generally, many rules of corporate law are decidedly second-best. That is, they are optimal only in recognition of the difficulties of enforcing any alternative rule. Agency problems can be reduced. They can never be eliminated.

Chapter 3. Shareholder Voting

Shareholders vote to elect the board and to approve fundamental changes, such as charter amendments (cf. DGCL 242(b)) or mergers (cf. DGCL 252(c)). Other matters *may* be submitted to a shareholder vote.

1. "Shareholder democracy"

Shareholder voting is often labeled "shareholder democracy." It differs considerably, however, from political elections in contemporary democracies such as the U.S.

First, the default rule in corporations is one vote per share ("one share one vote"), rather than one vote per shareholder (cf. DGCL 212(a)). Moreover, the corporate charter can authorize the issue of shares with different voting rights (DGCL 151(a)), which corporations such as Google, Facebook, or Snap have done: their founders hold high-voting stock, whereas outside investors hold low- or non-voting stock, such that the founders can maintain control even after selling a majority of the equity (measured by cash flow rights) to outside investors.

Second, voting rights are determined on the "record date," 10-60 days *before* the actual vote (DGCL 213). At least in practice, one keeps one's voting rights even if one sells the shares in between. (Any problem with this?)

Third, incumbents enjoy a large advantage. They control the voting process, and the corporation pays for their campaign.

Fourth, rational apathy is more pronounced in shareholder voting than in (national) political elections. In large corporations with dispersed ownership, an individual small shareholder has practically no influence on the outcome. It is thus rational for the shareholder not to spend time and resources learning about the issues at stake ("rational apathy"). So-called institutional investors such as pension funds or mutual funds might have more influence but their decision-makers lack the incentive to use it: The decision-makers are the funds' managers, but the benefits of higher share value accrue primarily to the funds' beneficiaries. (You might think that a fund manager benefits indirectly by attracting more new customers if the fund generates a higher return for existing customers. This is true for some idiosyncratic funds. But many funds, particularly index funds, invest in the same assets as their competitors and are evaluated relative to one another. The only way such funds can distinguish themselves from their competitors is through lower costs. For these funds, spending resources on voting *hurts* their competitive position relative to passive competitors even if the voting does lead to higher asset values.)

2. Voting rules and frequency

Unless otherwise provided in the charter or the statute, a majority of the shares entitled to vote constitutes a quorum (DGCL 216.1), and the affirmative vote of a majority of the shares present is required to pass a resolution (DGCL 216.2). The default for director elections is different (plurality voting, DGCL 216.3), but most large corporations have instituted some form of majority voting rule for director elections as well. This matters mostly when shareholders express their dissatisfaction through a "withhold campaign" against a particular director. Under the default rule, the director could be elected with a single vote (if running unopposed, as is the norm).

A more radical but rare deviation from the default rule is cumulative voting. See DGCL 214 for the technical details. Roughly, cumulative voting ensures proportional representation. Cf. *eBay v. Newmark* later in the course.

The corporation must hold a stockholder meeting at least once a year, DGCL 211(b). Under the default rules, only the board can call additional meetings (DGCL 211(a)(1)); shareholders may act instead by written consent (DGCL 228), but even that possibility is usually excluded in the charters of public corporations.

By default, all board seats are up for election every year. Under DGCL 141(d), however, the charter or a qualified bylaw can provide that as few as one third of the seats are contestable each year, i.e., that directors hold staggered terms of up to three years. This so-called "staggered board" probably seems like technical minutiae to you now. But it turns out to be an extremely important provision because it may critically delay anybody's attempt to take control of the board. We will first see this in *Blasius*. An important complementing rule is that unlike annually-elected boards, staggered boards are subject to removal only for cause (DGCL 141(k)(1); cf. DGCL 141(k)(2) for the case of cumulative voting).

3. Proxies

In principle, shareholders still vote at a physical "meeting" (but see the possibility of action by written consent, DGCL 228). But in large corporations, few shareholders attend such meetings in person, and those who do may not be the most important ones. Instead, shareholders vote by mail — sort of. U.S. corporations do not mail shareholders a proper ballot. Instead, the board solicits "proxies" on behalf of, and paid by, the corporation. Shareholders "vote" by granting or withholding proxies, and by choosing between any options that the proxy card may provide.

A proxy is a power of attorney to vote a shareholder's shares (cf. DGCL 212(b) — cf. sample card at https://goo.gl/nPJfEx (2nd last page)). The board solicits proxies on behalf of the corporation to ensure a quorum, to prevent a "coup" by a minority stockholder, and because the stock-exchange rules require it (see, e.g., NYSE Listed Company Manual 402.04). The board decides which proposals and nominees to include on the corporation's proxy card, with the exception of SEC proxy rule 14a-8, which allows shareholders to submit certain proposals for the corporation's proxy card (see below). The corporation pays.

Occasionally, "dissidents" solicit their own proxies in opposition to the incumbent board, usually in order to elect their own candidates to the board. This is called a proxy fight or proxy contest. However, proxy fights are very rare. Shareholders face a considerable collective action problem. The soliciting shareholder bears the entire cost of the solicitation, while receiving only a fraction of any benefit created.

This explains why it is so important who or what gets onto the corporation's proxy card. If it's not on the corporation's card, it won't receive any votes at the meeting, even if properly moved during the meeting. As far as the board is concerned, that's not a problem. They'll put onto the corporation's card whatever resolution and candidate they support. By contrast, challengers must rely on the law to get their proposals onto the corporation's card, otherwise boards happily reject the challengers' proposals. This is called "proxy access," and is discussed further in the "Proxy Access" section below.

4. The federal proxy rules

Proxy solicitations are heavily regulated by the SEC's proxy rules (Regulation 14A promulgated under section 14 of the Securities Exchange Act). As a result, the rules of corporate voting in the U.S. are a complicated interaction of federal proxy rules, state law, and a corporation's bylaws and charter.

The federal proxy rules are tedious. I provide a guide at simplifiedcodes.com. For a first course on corporations, you only need to know the following:

1. Before any proxy solicitation commences, a proxy statement must be filed with the SEC (rule 14a-6(b)). In contested matters, a preliminary proxy statement must be filed 10 days before any solicitation commences (rule 14a-6(a)).

2. The content and form of the proxy materials are heavily regulated (rules 14a-3, 14a–4, and 14a–5, and Schedule 14A). Virtually everything you see in an actual proxy statement is prescribed by the rules.

3. "Proxy" and "solicitation" are defined extremely broadly (rule 14a-1(f) and (l)(1)). Accordingly, the sweep of the proxy rules is very wide. In fact, in the past, the proxy rules impeded even conversations among shareholders about their votes. Certain exceptions to the definitions (particularly rule 14a-1(l)(2)(iv)) or requirements (particularly rules 14a-2(a)(6) and 14a-2(b)(1)-(3)) are therefore extremely important — you should read them.

4. Rule 14a-8 is the only federal rule requiring corporations to include shareholder proposals in the corporation's proxy materials. Under the rule, corporations must include in their proxy certain precatory resolutions and bylaw amendments sponsored by shareholders. By contrast, the rule does not cover director nominations or anything else that would affect "the upcoming election of directors" (see official note 8 to paragraph (i) of the rule). You should read the rule — unlike the rest of the proxy rules, it's written in plain English.

5. There is a special anti-fraud provision (rule 14a-9).

Questions

HLS Inc. has a single class of stock and three shareholders owning one third each: John M., John G., and Kristen S. Each shareholder is also a member of the current board. John M. currently serves as CEO. HLS Inc. generates about $10 million in annual profits; it has traditionally paid out all profits to the three shareholders every year.

Consider the following questions – what is the answer under the Delaware statute, not considering fiduciary duties (which will [fortunately] change many of the answers)?

1. Imagine that HLS Inc. is only subject to Delaware default rules, i.e., it does not have divergent charter provisions. Can John G. and Kristen S. do any or all of the following, in their capacity as shareholders and/or board members:

   Remove John M. from his position as CEO and his directorship, and instead elect their friend Jeannie S.—who does not own any stock in HLS Inc.—as a director and CEO.

   Issue new stock only to themselves and/or Jeannie S. at a low price.

   Cancel John M.'s stock.

   Pay dividends only to themselves (and Jeannie S. if she has become a shareholder).

   Stop paying dividends and instead pay out the profits as remuneration for "director services" and/or "CEO services" to themselves and/or Jeannie S., as applicable.

2. Now imagine that HLS Inc. has a staggered/classified board such that only one of the three directors is up for reelection each year (DGCL 141(d)). Does this possibly change any of your answers to Question 1?

3. Now imagine that HLS Inc. does not have a staggered board but dual class stock: John M. owns 50 shares of class A stock that has 10 votes per share, and John G. and Kristen S. each own 50 shares of class B stock that has 1 vote per share. Does this possibly change any of your answers to Question 1?

A. Schnell v. Chris-Craft Industries, Inc. (Del. 1971)

Questions

1. What is the basis for the Supreme Court's decision?
2. Does this basis constrain or at least guide the Supreme Court? Or can the Court do whatever it wants?

285 A.2d 437 (1971)

Andrew H. SCHNELL, Jr. and Jack Safer, Plaintiffs Below,
Appellants,

v.

CHRIS-CRAFT INDUSTRIES, INC., a Delaware corporation,
Defendant Below, Appellee.

Supreme Court of Delaware.
November 29, 1971.

H. Albert Young and Edward B. Maxwell, 2nd, of Young, Conaway, Stargatt & Taylor, Wilmington, and Carl F. Goodman, New York City, and Jay L. Westbrook, of Surrey, Karasik & Greene, Washington, D. C., for plaintiffs below, appellants.

David F. Anderson and Charles S. Crompton, Jr., of Potter, Anderson & Corroon, Wilmington, and Arthur L. Liman and Daniel P. Levitt, of Paul, Weiss, Rifkind, Wharton & Garrison, New York City, and Washington, D. C., for defendant below, appellee.

Before WOLCOTT, C.J., and CAREY and HERRMANN, Associate Justices: [438]

HERRMANN, Justice (for the majority of the Court):

This is an appeal from the denial by the Court of Chancery of the petition of dissident stockholders for injunctive relief to prevent management* from advancing the date of the annual stockholders' meeting from January 11, 1972, as previously set by the by-laws, to December 8, 1971.

The opinion below is reported at 285 A.2d 430. This opinion is confined to the frame of reference of the opinion below for the sake of brevity and because of the strictures of time imposed by the circumstances of the case.

---

* We use this word as meaning "managing directors".

[HS—The Chancellor had stated the most pertinent facts as follows:

Plaintiffs, who are stockholders of the defendant, seek a preliminary injunction against the carrying out by such corporation of a change in the date of its annual meeting of stockholders which was ostensibly accomplished by an amendment to its by-laws adopted at a directors' meeting held on October 18, 1971. As a result of such change in by-law and the fixing of a new date by the directors, such annual meeting is now scheduled to be held on December 8, 1971 instead of on the date fixed in the by-law in question before its amendment, namely the second Tuesday in January, 1972. Plaintiffs ... are dissatisfied with defendant's recent business performance ... Accordingly, they have embarked on a proxy contest against present management with the purpose in mind of electing new directors and installing new management at Chris-Craft. ... Plaintiffs contend that by advancing the date of defendant's annual meeting by over a month and by the selection of an allegedly isolated town in up-state New York as the place for such meeting, defendant's board has deliberately sought to handicap the efforts of plaintiffs and other stockholders sympathetic to plaintiffs' views adequately to place their case before their fellow stockholders for decision because of the exigencies of time.]

It will be seen that the Chancery Court considered all of the reasons stated by management as business reasons for changing the date of the meeting; but that those reasons were rejected by the Court below in making the following findings:

"I am satisfied, however, in a situation in which present management has disingenuously resisted the production of a list of its stockholders to plaintiffs or their confederates and has otherwise turned a deaf ear to plaintiffs' demands about a change in management designed to lift defendant from its present business [439] doldrums, management has seized on a relatively new section of the Delaware Corporation Law for the purpose of cutting down on the amount of time which would otherwise have been available to plaintiffs and others for the waging of a proxy battle. Management thus enlarged the scope of its scheduled October 18 directors' meeting to include the by-law amendment in controversy after the stockholders committee had filed with the S.E.C. its intention to wage a proxy fight on October 16.

"Thus plaintiffs reasonably contend that because of the tactics employed by management (which involve the hiring of two established proxy solicitors as well as a refusal to produce a list of its stockholders, coupled with its use of an amendment to the Delaware Corporation Law to limit the time for contest), they are given little chance, because of the exigencies of time, including that required to clear material at the S.E.C., to wage a successful proxy fight between now and December 8. * * *."

In our view, those conclusions amount to a finding that management has attempted to utilize the corporate machinery and the Delaware Law for the purpose of perpetuating itself in office; and, to that end, for the purpose of obstructing the legitimate efforts of dissident stockholders in the exercise of their rights to undertake a proxy contest against management. These are inequitable purposes, contrary to established principles of corporate democracy. The advancement by directors of the by-law date of a stockholders' meeting, for such purposes, may not be permitted to stand. Compare Condec Corporation v. Lunkenheimer Company, Del.Ch., 230 A.2d 769 (1967).

When the by-laws of a corporation designate the date of the annual meeting of stockholders, it is to be expected that those who intend to contest the reelection of incumbent management will gear their campaign to the by-law date. It is not to be expected that management will attempt to advance that date in order to obtain an inequitable advantage in the contest.

Management contends that it has complied strictly with the provisions of the new Delaware Corporation Law in changing the by-law date. The answer to that contention, of course, is that inequitable action does not become permissible simply because it is legally possible.

Management relies upon American Hardware Corp. v. Savage Arms Corp., 37 Del.Ch. 10, 135 A.2d 725, aff'd 37 Del.Ch. 59, 136 A.2d 690 (1957). That case is inapposite for two reasons: it involved an effort by stockholders, engaged in a proxy contest, to have the stockholders' meeting adjourned and the period for the proxy contest enlarged; and there was no finding there of inequitable action on the part of management. We agree with the rule of American Hardware that, in the absence of fraud or inequitable conduct, the date for a stockholders' meeting and notice thereof, duly established under the by-laws, will not be enlarged by judicial interference at the request of dissident stockholders solely because of the circumstance of a proxy contest. That, of course, is not the case before us.

We are unable to agree with the conclusion of the Chancery Court that the stockholders' application for injunctive relief here was tardy and came too late. The stockholders learned of the action of management unofficially on Wednesday, October 27, 1971; they filed this action on Monday, November 1, 1971. Until management changed the date of the meeting, the stockholders had no need of judicial assistance in that connection. There is no indication of any prior warning of management's intent to take such action; indeed, it appears that an attempt was made by management to conceal its action as long as possible. Moreover, stockholders may not be charged with the duty of anticipating inequitable action by management, and of seeking anticipatory injunctive relief to foreclose such action, simply because the [440] new Delaware Corporation Law makes such inequitable action legally possible.

Accordingly, the judgment below must be reversed and the cause remanded, with instructions to nullify the December 8 date as a meeting date for stockholders; to reinstate January 11, 1972 as the sole date of the next annual meeting of the stockholders of the corporation; and to take such other proceedings and action as may be consistent herewith regarding the stock record closing date and any other related matters.

WOLCOTT, Chief Justice (dissenting):

I do not agree with the majority of the Court in its disposition of this appeal. The plaintiff stockholders concerned in this litigation have, for a considerable period of time, sought to obtain control of the defendant corporation. These attempts took various forms.

In view of the length of time leading up to the immediate events which caused the filing of this action, I agree with the Vice Chancellor that the application for injunctive relief came too late.

I would affirm the judgment below on the basis of the Vice Chancellor's opinion.

B. Blasius Industries, Inc. v. Atlas Corp. (Del. Ch. 1988)

Blasius is the classic Chancery Court decision applying, and expanding on, *Schnell*.

I edit this case more than usual because it involves M&A issues and terminology that we will only learn later in the course. For present purposes, it is enough to understand that Blasius attempted to get its people elected to the Atlas board, and that Atlas's management did not like this at all.

Questions

3. Is the vote at issue a normal vote taken at a meeting?

4. What did the Atlas board do to frustrate the vote, and why would that work?

5. What exactly does Chancellor Allen have to say about corporate voting—what is it about voting that is important?

6. Does Allen's discussion of voting, its importance, and its judicial treatment matter for the ultimate outcome of the case here?

7. If not, why would he have bothered?

564 A.2d 651 (1988)

BLASIUS INDUSTRIES, INC., [...]

v.

ATLAS CORPORATION, [...]

Court of Chancery of Delaware, New Castle County.

Submitted: June 6, 1988.

Decided: July 25, 1988.

[...]

OPINION

ALLEN, Chancellor.

Two cases pitting the directors of Atlas Corporation against that company's largest (9.1%) shareholder, Blasius Industries, have been consolidated and tried together. Together, these cases ultimately require the court to determine who is entitled to sit on Atlas' board of directors. Each, however, presents discrete and important legal issues.

The first of the cases was filed on December 30, 1987. As amended, it challenges the validity of board action taken at a telephone meeting of December 31, 1987 that added two new members to Atlas' seven member board. That action was taken as an immediate response to the delivery to Atlas by Blasius the previous day of a form of stockholder consent that, if joined in by holders of a majority of Atlas' stock, would have increased the board of Atlas from seven to fifteen members and would have elected eight new members nominated by Blasius.

As I find the facts of this first case, they present the question whether a board acts consistently with its fiduciary duty when it acts, in good faith and with appropriate care, for the primary purpose of preventing or impeding an unaffiliated majority of shareholders from expanding the board and electing a new majority. For the reasons that follow, I conclude that, even though defendants here acted on their view of the corporation's interest and not selfishly, their December 31 action constituted an offense to the relationship between corporate directors and shareholders that has traditionally been protected in courts of equity. As a consequence, I conclude that the board action taken on December 31 was invalid and must be voided. The basis for this opinion is set forth at pages 658-663 below.

The second filed action was commenced on March 9, 1988. It arises out of the consent solicitation itself (or an amended [653] version of it) and requires the court to determine the outcome of Blasius' consent solicitation, which was warmly and actively contested on both sides. The vote was, on either view of the facts and law, extremely close. For the reasons set forth at pages 663-670 below, I conclude that the judges of election properly confined their count to the written "ballots" (so to speak) before them; that on that basis, they made several errors, but that correction of those errors does not reverse the result they announced. I therefore conclude that plaintiffs' consent solicitation failed to garner the support of a majority of Atlas shares.

The facts set forth below represent findings based upon a preponderance of the admissible evidence, as I evaluate it.

I.

Blasius Acquires a 9% Stake in Atlas.

Blasius is a new stockholder of Atlas. It began to accumulate Atlas shares for the first time in July, 1987. On October 29, it filed a Schedule 13D with the Securities Exchange Commission disclosing that, with affiliates, it then owed 9.1% of Atlas' common stock.[♦] It stated in that filing that it intended to encourage management of Atlas to consider a restructuring of the Company or other transaction to enhance shareholder values. It

♦ Under section 13(d) of the Securities Exchange Act, anyone acquiring 5% of (any class of) a corporation's voting stock must within ten days file a Schedule 13D disclosing this and any subsequent acquisitions. This rule applies only to "registered equity securities," but any publicly traded stock must be registered.

◆◆ Tender offer = an offer to purchase shares addressed to all shareholders

◆◆◆ Leveraged buyout (LBO) = a purchase financed largely with debt. The debt is usually secured by the purchased corporation's assets. LBOs became frequent and spectacularly large in the 1980s. For the LBO to succeed post-acquisition, the target corporation must produce high and steady cash flows to service the high levels of debt incurred. Otherwise, the target will end up in bankruptcy. We will discuss these issues in much greater detail later in the course.

also disclosed that Blasius was exploring the feasibility of obtaining control of Atlas, including instituting a tender offer◆◆ or seeking "appropriate" representation on the Atlas board of directors.

Blasius has recently come under the control of two individuals, Michael Lubin and Warren Delano, who after experience in the commercial banking industry, had, for a short time, run a venture capital operation for a small investment banking firm. Now on their own, they apparently came to control Blasius with the assistance of Drexel Burnham's well noted junk bond mechanism. Since then, they have made several attempts to effect leveraged buyouts,◆◆◆ but without success.

In May, 1987, with Drexel Burnham serving as underwriter, Lubin and Delano caused Blasius to raise $60 million through the sale of junk bonds. A portion of these funds were used to acquire a 9% position in Atlas. According to its public filings with the SEC, Blasius' debt service obligations arising out of the sale of the junk bonds are such that it is unable to service those obligations from its income from operations.

The prospect of Messrs. Lubin and Delano involving themselves in Atlas' affairs, was not a development welcomed by Atlas' management. Atlas had a new CEO, defendant Weaver, who [...] wrote in his diary on October 30, 1987:

> 13D by Delano & Lubin came in today. Had long conversation w/MAH & Mark Golden [of Goldman, Sachs] on issue. All agree we must dilute these people down by the acquisition of another Co. w/stock, or merger or something else.

The Blasius Proposal of A Leverage Recapitalization Or Sale.

Immediately after filing its 13D on October 29, Blasius' representatives sought a meeting with the Atlas management. Atlas dragged its feet. A meeting was arranged for December 2, 1987 following the regular meeting of the Atlas board. Attending that meeting were Messrs. Lubin and Delano for Blasius, and, for Atlas, Messrs. Weaver, Devaney (Atlas' CFO), Masinter (legal counsel and director) and Czajkowski (a representative of Atlas' investment banker, Goldman Sachs).

[654] At that meeting, Messrs. Lubin and Delano suggested that Atlas engage in a leveraged restructuring and distribute cash to shareholders. In such a transaction, which is by this date a commonplace form of transaction, a corporation typically raises cash by sale of assets and significant borrowings and makes a large one time cash distribution to shareholders. The shareholders are typically left with cash and an equity interest in a

smaller, more highly leveraged enterprise. Lubin and Delano gave the outline of a leveraged recapitalization for Atlas as they saw it.

Immediately following the meeting, the Atlas representatives expressed among themselves an initial reaction that the proposal was infeasible. On December 7, Mr. Lubin sent a letter detailing the proposal. [...]

Atlas Asks Its Investment Banker to Study the Proposal.

This written proposal was distributed to the Atlas board on December 9 and Goldman Sachs was directed to review and analyze it.

[...]

Blasius attempted on December 14 and December 22 to arrange a further meeting with the Atlas management without success. During this period, Atlas provided Goldman Sachs with projections for the Company. Lubin was told that a further meeting would await completion of Goldman's analysis. A meeting after the first of the year was proposed.

The Delivery of Blasius' Consent Statement.

On December 30, 1987, Blasius caused Cede & Co. (the registered owner of its Atlas stock) to deliver to Atlas a signed written consent (1) adopting a precatory resolution recommending that the board develop and implement a restructuring proposal, (2) amending the Atlas bylaws to, among other things, expand the size of the board from seven to fifteen members — the maximum number under Atlas' charter, and (3) electing eight named persons to fill the new directorships. Blasius also filed suit that day in this court seeking a declaration that certain bylaws adopted by the board on September 1, 1987 acted as an unlawful restraint on the shareholders' right, created by Section 228 of our corporation statute, to act through consent without undergoing a meeting.

The reaction was immediate. Mr. Weaver conferred with Mr. Masinter, the Company's outside counsel and a director, who viewed the consent as an attempt to take control of the Company. They decided to call an emergency meeting of the board, even though a regularly scheduled meeting was to occur only one week hence, on January [655] 6, 1988. The point of the emergency meeting was to act on their conclusion (or to seek to have the board act on their conclusion) "that we should add at least one and probably two directors to the board ..." (Tr. 85, Vol. II). A quorum of directors, however, could not be arranged for a telephone meeting that day. A telephone meeting was held the next day. At that meeting, the board voted to amend the bylaws to increase the size of the board from seven to nine and appointed John M. Devaney and Harry J. Winters, Jr. to fill those newly created positions. Atlas' Certificate of Incorporation creates staggered terms for directors; the terms to which Messrs. Devaney and Winters were appointed would expire in 1988 and 1990, respectively.

The Motivation of the Incumbent Board In Expanding the Board and Appointing New Members.

In increasing the size of Atlas' board by two and filling the newly created positions, the members of the board realized that they were thereby precluding the holders of a majority of the Company's shares from placing a majority of new directors on the board through Blasius' consent solicitation, should they want to do so. Indeed the evidence establishes that that was the principal motivation in so acting.

The conclusion that, in creating two new board positions on December 31 and electing Messrs. Devaney and Winters to fill those positions the board was principally motivated to prevent or delay the shareholders from possibly placing a majority of new members on the board, is critical to my analysis of the central issue posed by the first filed of the two pending cases. If the board in fact was not so motivated, but rather had taken action completely independently of the consent solicitation, which merely had an incidental impact upon the possible effectuation of any action authorized by the shareholders, it is very unlikely that such action would be subject to judicial nullification. *See, e.g., Frantz Manufacturing Company v. EAC Industries,* Del.Supr., 501 A.2d 401, 407 (1985); *Moran v. Household International, Inc.,* Del.Ch., 490 A.2d 1059, 1080, *aff'd,* Del. Supr., 500 A.2d 1346 (1985). The board, as a general matter, is under no fiduciary obligation to suspend its active management of the firm while the consent solicitation process goes forward.

There is testimony in the record to support the proposition that, in acting on December 31, the board was principally motivated simply to implement a plan to expand the Atlas board that preexisted the September, 1987 emergence of Blasius as an active shareholder. I have no doubt that the addition of Mr. Winters, an expert in mining economics, and Mr. Devaney, a financial expert employed by the Company, strengthened the Atlas board and, should anyone ever have reason to review the wisdom of those choices, they would be found to be sensible and prudent. I cannot conclude, however, that the strengthening of the board by the addition of these men was the principal motive for the December 31 action. As I view this factual determination as critical, I will pause to dilate briefly upon the evidence that leads me to this conclusion.

The evidence indicates that CEO Weaver was acquainted with Mr. Winters prior to the time he assumed the presidency of Atlas. When, in the fall of 1986, Mr. Weaver learned of his selection as Atlas' future CEO, he informally approached Mr. Winters about serving on the board of the Company. Winters indicated a willingness to do so and sent to Mr. Weaver a copy of his *curriculum vitae.* Weaver, however, took no action with respect to this matter until he had some informal discussion with other board members on December 2, 1987, the date on which Mr. Lubin orally presented Blasius' restructuring proposal to management. At that time, he mentioned the possibility to other board members.

Then, on December 7, Mr. Weaver called Mr. Winters on the telephone and asked him if he would serve on the board and Mr. Winters again agreed.

On December 24, 1987, Mr. Weaver wrote to other board members, sending them Mr. Winters *curriculum vitae* and notifying them that Mr. Winters would be [656] proposed for board membership at the forthcoming January 6 meeting. It was also suggested that a dinner meeting be scheduled for January 5, in order to give board members who did not know Mr. Winters an opportunity to meet him prior to acting on that suggestion. The addition of Mr. Devaney to the board was not mentioned in that memo, nor, so far as the record discloses, was it discussed at the December 2 board meeting.

It is difficult to consider the timing of the activation of the interest in adding Mr. Winters to the board in December as simply coincidental with the pressure that Blasius was applying. The connection between the two events, however, becomes unmistakably clear when the later events of December 30 and 31 are focused upon. As noted above, on the 30th, Atlas received the Blasius consent which proposed to shareholders that they expand the board from seven to fifteen and add eight new members identified in the consent. It also proposed the adoption of a precatory resolution encouraging restructuring or sale of the Company. Mr. Weaver immediately met with Mr. Masinter. In addition to receiving the consent, Atlas was informed it had been sued in this court, but it did not yet know the thrust of that action. At that time, Messrs. Weaver and Masinter "discussed a lot of [reactive] strategies and Edgar [Masinter] told me we really got to put a program together to go forward with this consent.... we talked about taking no action. We talked about adding one board member. We talked about adding two board members. We talked about adding eight board members. And we did a lot of looking at other and various and sundry alternatives...." (Weaver Testimony, Tr. I, p. 130). They decided to add two board members and to hold an emergency board meeting that very day to do so. It is clear that the reason that Mr. Masinter advised taking this step immediately rather than waiting for the January 6 meeting was that he feared that the Court of Chancery might issue a temporary restraining order prohibiting the board from increasing its membership, since the consent solicitation had commenced. It is admitted that there was no fear that Blasius would be in a position to complete a public solicitation for consents prior to the January 6 board meeting.

In this setting, I conclude that, while the addition of these qualified men would, under other circumstances, be clearly appropriate as an independent step, such a step was in fact taken in order to impede or preclude a majority of the shareholders from effectively adopting the course proposed by Blasius. Indeed, while defendants never forsake the factual argument that that action was simply a continuation of business as usual, they, in effect, admit from time to time this overriding purpose. For example, everyone concedes that the directors understood on December 31 that the effect of adding two directors would be to preclude stockholders from effectively implementing the Blasius proposal. Mr. Weaver, for example, testifies as follows:

> Q: Was it your view that by electing these two directors, Atlas was preventing Blasius from electing a majority of the board?

> A: I think that is a component of my total overview. I think in the short term, yes, it did.

Directors Farley and Bongiovanni admit that the board acted to slow the Blasius proposal down. *See* Tr. T, Vol. I, at pp. 23-24 and 81.

This candor is praiseworthy, but any other statement would be frankly incredible. The timing of these events is, in my opinion, consistent only with the conclusion that Mr. Weaver and Mr. Masinter originated, and the board immediately endorsed, the notion of adding these competent, friendly individuals to the board, not because the board felt an urgent need to get them on the board immediately for reasons relating to the operations of Atlas' business, but because to do so would, for the moment, preclude a majority of shareholders from electing eight new board members selected by Blasius. As explained below, I conclude that, in so acting, the board was not selfishly motivated simply to retain power.

There was no discussion at the December 31 meeting of the feasibility or wisdom of the Blasius restructuring proposal. While [657] several of the directors had an initial impression that the plan was not feasible and, if implemented, would likely result in the eventual liquidation of the Company, they had not yet focused upon and acted on that subject. Goldman Sachs had not yet made its report, which was scheduled to be given January 6.

The January 6 Rejection of the Blasius Proposal.

On January 6, the board convened for its scheduled meeting. At that time, it heard a full report from its financial advisor concerning the feasibility of the Blasius restructuring proposal. [...]

The board then voted to reject the Blasius proposal. Blasius was informed of that action. The next day, Blasius caused a second, modified consent to be delivered to Atlas. A contest then ensued between the Company and Blasius for the votes of Atlas' shareholders. The facts relating to that contest, and a determination of its outcome, form the subject of the second filed lawsuit to be now decided. That matter, however, will be deferred for the moment as the facts set forth above are sufficient to frame and decide the principal remaining issue raised by the first filed action: whether the December 31 board action, in increasing the board by two and appointing members to fill those new positions, constituted, in the circumstances, an inequitable interference with the exercise of shareholder rights.

II.

Plaintiff attacks the December 31 board action as a selfishly motivated effort to protect the incumbent board from a perceived threat to its control of Atlas. Their conduct is said to constitute a violation of the principle, applied in such cases as *Schnell v. Chris Craft Industries*, Del. Supr., 285 A.2d 437 (1971), that directors hold legal powers subjected to a supervening duty to exercise such powers in good faith pursuit of what they reasonably believe to be in the corporation's interest. The December 31 action is also said to have been taken in a grossly negligent manner, since it was designed to preclude the recapitalization from being pursued, and the board had no basis at that time to make a prudent determination about the wisdom of that proposal, nor was there any emergency that required it to act in any respect regarding that proposal before putting itself in a position to do so advisedly.

Defendants, of course, contest every aspect of plaintiffs' claims. They claim the formidable protections of the business judgment rule. *See, e.g., Aronson v. Lewis,* Del.Supr., 473 A.2d 805 (1983); *Grobow v. Perot,* Del.Supr., 539 A.2d 180 (1988); *In re J.P. Stevens & Co., Inc. Shareholders Litigation,* Del.Ch., 542 A.2d 770 (1988).

They say that, in creating two new board positions and filling them on December 31, they acted without a conflicting interest [658] (since the Blasius proposal did not, in any event, challenge *their* places on the board), they acted with due care (since they well knew the persons they put on the board and did not thereby preclude later consideration of the recapitalization), and they acted in good faith (since they were motivated, they say, to protect the shareholders from the threat of having an impractical, indeed a dangerous, recapitalization program foisted upon them). Accordingly, defendants assert there is no basis to conclude that their December 31 action constituted any violation of the duty of the fidelity that a director owes by reason of his office to the corporation and its shareholders.

[...]

III.

One of the principal thrusts of plaintiffs' argument is that, in acting to appoint two additional persons of their own selection, including an officer of the Company, to the board, defendants were motivated not by any view that Atlas' interest (or those of its shareholders) required that action, but rather they were motivated improperly, by selfish concern to maintain their collective control over the Company. That is, plaintiffs say that the evidence shows there was no policy dispute or issue that really motivated this action, but that asserted policy differences were pretexts for entrenchment for selfish reasons. If this were found to be factually true, one would not need to inquire further. The action taken would constitute a breach of duty. *Schnell v. Chris Craft Industries,* Del.Supr., 285 A.2d 437 (1971); *Guiricich v. Emtrol Corp.,* Del.Supr., 449 A.2d 232 (1982).

In support of this view, plaintiffs point to the early diary entry of Mr. Weaver (p. 653, *supra*), to the lack of any consideration at all of the Blasius recapitalization proposal at the December 31 meeting, the lack of any substantial basis for the outside directors to have had any considered view on the subject by that time — not having had any view from Goldman Sachs nor seen the financial data that it regarded as necessary to evaluate the proposal — and upon what it urges is the grievously flawed, slanted analysis that Goldman Sachs finally did present.

While I am satisfied that the evidence is powerful, indeed compelling, that the board was chiefly motivated on December 31 to forestall or preclude the possibility that a majority of shareholders might place on the Atlas board eight new members sympathetic to the Blasius proposal, it is less clear with respect to the more subtle motivational question: whether the existing members of the board did so because they held a good faith belief that such shareholder action would be self-injurious and shareholders needed to be protected from their own judgment.

On balance, I cannot conclude that the board was acting out of a self-interested motive in any important respect on December 31. I conclude rather that the board saw the "threat" of the Blasius recapitalization proposal as posing vital policy differences between itself and Blasius. It acted, I conclude, in a good faith effort to protect its incumbency, not selfishly, but in order to thwart implementation of the recapitalization that it feared, reasonably, would cause great injury to the Company.

The real question the case presents, to my mind, is whether, in these circumstances, the board, even if it *is* acting with subjective good faith (which will typically, if not always, be a contestable or debatable judicial conclusion), may validly act for the principal purpose of preventing the shareholders from electing a majority of new directors. The question thus posed is not one of intentional wrong (or even negligence), but one of authority *as between the fiduciary and the beneficiary* (not simply [659] legal authority, *i.e.*, as between the fiduciary and the world at large).

IV.

[...]

1. Why the deferential business judgment rule does not apply to board acts taken for the primary purpose of interfering with a stockholder's vote, even if taken advisedly and in good faith.

A. The question of legitimacy.

The shareholder franchise is the ideological underpinning upon which the legitimacy of directorial power rests. Generally, shareholders have only two protections against perceived inadequate business performance. They may sell their stock (which, if done in sufficient numbers, may so affect security prices as to create an incentive for altered managerial performance), or they may vote to replace incumbent board members.

It has, for a long time, been conventional to dismiss the stockholder vote as a vestige or ritual of little practical importance.[...] It may be that we are now witnessing the emergence of new institutional voices and arrangements that will make the stockholder vote a less predictable affair than it has been. Be that as it may, however, whether the vote is seen functionally as an unimportant formalism, or as an important tool of discipline, it is clear that it is critical to the theory that legitimates the exercise of power by some (directors and officers) over vast aggregations of property that they do not own. Thus, when viewed from a broad, institutional perspective, it can be seen that matters involving the integrity of the shareholder voting process involve consideration not present in any other context in which directors exercise delegated power.

B. Questions of this type raise issues of the allocation of authority as between the board and the shareholders.

The distinctive nature of the shareholder franchise context also appears when the matter is viewed from a less generalized, doctrinal point of view. From this point of view, as well, it appears that the ordinary considerations to which the business judgment rule originally responded are simply not present in the shareholder voting context.[2] That is, a decision by

---

[2] A similar concern, for credible corporate democracy, underlies those cases that strike down board action that sets or moves an annual meeting date upon a finding that such action was intended to thwart a shareholder group from effectively mounting an election campaign. *See, e.g., Schnell v. Chris Craft,* [...]

the [660] board to act for the primary purpose of preventing the effectiveness of a shareholder vote inevitably involves the question who, as between the principal and the agent, has authority with respect to a matter of internal corporate governance. That, of course, is true in a very specific way in this case which deals with the question who should constitute the board of directors of the corporation, but it will be true in every instance in which an incumbent board seeks to thwart a shareholder majority. A board's decision to act to prevent the shareholders from creating a majority of new board positions and filling them does not involve the exercise of *the corporation's power* over its property, or with respect to *its* rights or obligations; rather, it involves allocation, between shareholders as a class and the board, of effective power with respect to governance of the corporation. This need not be the case with respect to other forms of corporate action that may have an entrenchment effect [...] Action designed principally to interfere with the effectiveness of a vote inevitably involves a conflict between the board and a shareholder majority. Judicial review of such action involves a determination of the legal and equitable obligations of an agent towards his principal. This is not, in my opinion, a question that a court may leave to the agent finally to decide so long as he does so honestly and competently; that is, it may not be left to the agent's business judgment. [...]

2. What rule does apply: per se invalidity of corporate acts intended primarily to thwart effective exercise of the franchise or is there an intermediate standard?

Plaintiff argues for a rule of *per se* invalidity once a plaintiff has established that a board has acted for the primary purpose of thwarting the exercise of a shareholder vote. [...]

A *per se* rule that would strike down, in equity, any board action taken for the primary purpose of interfering with the effectiveness of a corporate vote would have the advantage of relative clarity and predictability. It also has the advantage of most vigorously enforcing the concept of corporate democracy. The disadvantage it brings along is, of course, the disadvantage a *per se* rule always has: it may sweep too broadly.

[...]

In my view, our inability to foresee now all of the future settings in which a board might, in good faith, paternalistically seek to thwart a shareholder vote, counsels against the adoption of a *per se* rule invalidating, in equity, every board action taken for the sole or

---

The cases invalidating stock issued for the primary purpose of diluting the voting power of a control block also reflect the law's concern that a credible form of corporate democracy be maintained. [...]

Similarly, a concern for corporate democracy is reflected (1) in our statutory requirement of annual meetings (8 *Del.C.* § 211), and in the cases that aggressively and summarily enforce that right [...,] and (2) in our consent statute (8 *Del.C.* § 228) and the interpretation it has been accorded.

primary purpose of thwarting a shareholder vote, even though I recognize the transcending significance of the franchise to the claims to legitimacy of our scheme of corporate governance. It may be that some set of facts would justify such extreme action. [...] This, however, is not such a case.

3. Defendants have demonstrated no sufficient justification for the action of December 31 which was intended to prevent an unaffiliated majority of shareholders from effectively exercising their right to elect eight new directors.

The board was not faced with a coercive action taken by a powerful shareholder against the interests of a distinct shareholder constituency (such as a public minority). It was presented with a consent [663] solicitation by a 9% shareholder. Moreover, here it had time (and understood that it had time) to inform the shareholders of its views on the merits of the proposal subject to stockholder vote. The only justification that can, in such a situation, be offered for the action taken is that the board knows better than do the shareholders what is in the corporation's best interest. While that premise is no doubt true for any number of matters, it is irrelevant (except insofar as the shareholders wish to be guided by the board's recommendation) when the question is who should comprise the board of directors. The theory of our corporation law confers power upon directors as the agents of the shareholders; it does not create Platonic masters. It may be that the Blasius restructuring proposal was or is unrealistic and would lead to injury to the corporation and its shareholders if pursued. Having heard the evidence, I am inclined to think it was not a sound proposal. The board certainly viewed it that way, and that view, held in good faith, entitled the board to take certain steps to evade the risk it perceived. It could, for example, expend corporate funds to inform shareholders and seek to bring them to a similar point of view. *See, e.g. Hall v. Trans-Lux Daylight Picture Screen Corporation*, Del.Ch., 171 A. 226, 227 (1934); *Hibbert v. Hollywood Park, Inc.*, Del. Supr., 457 A.2d 339 (1982). But there is a vast difference between expending corporate funds to inform the electorate and exercising power for the primary purpose of foreclosing effective shareholder action. A majority of the shareholders, who were not dominated in any respect, could view the matter differently than did the board. If they do, or did, they are entitled to employ the mechanisms provided by the corporation law and the Atlas certificate of incorporation to advance that view. They are also entitled, in my opinion, to restrain their agents, the board, from acting for the principal purpose of thwarting that action.

I therefore conclude that, even finding the action taken was taken in good faith, it constituted an unintended violation of the duty of loyalty that the board owed to the shareholders. I note parenthetically that the concept of an unintended breach of the duty of loyalty is unusual but not novel. *See Lerman v. Diagnostic Data, supra; AC Acquisitions Corp. v. Anderson, Clayton & Co.*, Del.Ch., 519 A.2d 103 (1986). That action will, therefore, be set aside by order of this court.

V.

I turn now to a discussion of the second case which is a Section 225 case designed to determine whether the nominees of Blasius were elected to an expanded Atlas board pursuant to the consent procedure. [...]

On March 6, 1988, after several rounds of mailings by each side, Blasius presented consents to the corporation purporting to adopt its five proposals. The corporation appointed an independent fiduciary (Manufacturers Hanover Trust Company) to act as judge of the stockholder vote. It reported a final tally report on March 17 and issued a Certificate of the Stockholder Vote on March 22. That certificate stated that the vote had been exceedingly close and that, as calculated by Manufacturer's Hanover, none of Blasius' proposals had succeeded. In order to be adopted by a majority of shares entitled to vote, each proposition needed to garner 1,486,293 consents. Each was about 45,000 shares short (about 1.5% of the total outstanding stock). [...]

VI.

The multilevel system of beneficial ownership of stock and the interposition of other institutional players between investors and corporations (*e.g.*, [...] brokers whose customers hold stock beneficially) renders the process of corporate voting complex. This case demonstrates that the currently employed process by which consents are solicited and counted is even more prone to problems than is the process of proxy counting. [...]

There were mistakes made by the judges [...] and by record owners and their agents; there appears to have been unauthorized and perhaps even wrongful behavior (*e.g.*, B.C. Christopher & Co.). Much of the problem arises from the perhaps thoughtless utilization of proxy contest procedures for a consent solicitation contest. But the mistakes of the judges, on balance, tend to cut against plaintiff. [...]

We cannot know, in these circumstances, what the outcome of this close contest would have been if the true wishes of all beneficial owners had been accurately measured. The parties must, in my opinion, be content with the result announced by the judges. Those mistakes that were made by the judges do not alter the outcome.

Judgment will be entered in favor of defendants. [...]

C. Proxy Access

Proxy access has been the most contested corporate governance regulation for over a decade. Proxy access means the ability of shareholders to have one or more shareholder nominees included on *the corporation's* proxy card.

In this millennium, the SEC first proposed formal rules dealing with proxy access in 2003 and 2007. In 2009, the SEC again proposed to require proxy access in a new rule 14a-11. In response, it received about 700 comments. The comments were sharply divided on the merits of the proposed rule. Major corporations and their law firms opposed it, whereas institutional investors supported it. Congress weighed in with Section 971 of the Dodd-Frank Act of 2010, which amended section 14 of the Securities Exchange Act to give the SEC explicit authority to require proxy access. The SEC ultimately adopted a modified rule 14a-11 in 2010. In Business Roundtable v. SEC (2011), however, the D.C. Circuit struck down this new rule as "arbitrary and capricious" under the Administrative Procedure Act. Judge Ginsburg's opinion is noticeable for its hostility towards the SEC and its strict demands of cost-benefit analysis. The SEC seems intent on trying it again, but has not mustered the resources to do so yet.

1. Why might proxy access matter?: The shareholder collective action problem

As you know, shareholders have the right to nominate director candidates and to solicit proxies to vote for them. But under the default rules, shareholders do not have the right to have these candidates included in *the corporation's* proxy materials, which are mailed and paid for by the corporation. (What about rule 14a-8?) Nor do shareholders have the right to be reimbursed for their costs of running their own proxy campaign (hundreds of thousands or even millions of dollars). The board *may* reimburse a challenger's cost if the contest was about corporate policy rather than mere personnel issues. But realistically, no incumbent board will do so. The only practical way for a challenger to be reimbursed is to win control of the board.

Given these costs, shareholder opposition faces a considerable collective action problem. An activist shareholder would need to spend a lot of money to run a proxy fight, yet reap only a fraction of the returns.

Let's look at the incentives in a simple numerical example. Imagine better management could increase the value of a corporation's shares by $100m (say, from $1 billion to $1.1 billion). You own 1% of those shares. Your individual benefit from better management would hence be $1m. Let's say a proxy contest would cost $2m.

If you win and replace the board, your candidates will vote to reimburse you. You will hence make a $1m gain because your shares are worth more with better management. But if you lose, you won't be reimbursed, your shares' value does not appreciate, and you are stuck with the $2m costs.

Imagine the chances of winning the proxy contest are 50-50 (in practice, that's high — people tend to be suspicious of insurgents). In expectation, you would lose $500,000 (50% × $1m – 50% × $2m = -$500,000). Thus, you won't do it. And this happens even though in this example (1) you own $10m worth of shares of this one corporation— a big stake for most investors, and (2) the expected collective benefit to all shareholders combined is $48m (50% × $100m - $2m = $48m).

2. Variations in the bylaws or the charter

As usual, these default rules can be changed in the charter (cf. DGCL 102(b)(1)) or in the bylaws (cf. DGCL 109). Details of permissible bylaws were disputed, prompting the adoption of DGCL 112 and 113 in 2009 (read!).

Shareholders can use bylaw amendments to obtain the right to proxy access and/or to proxy expense reimbursement even against the opposition of the board (why can shareholders not use charter amendments for this purpose?). And SEC rule 14a-8 allows them to collect "votes" for such amendments using the corporation's proxy. Rule 14a-8(i)(8) excludes director nominations from 14a-8, but it does not exclude bylaw proposals relating to such nominations in subsequent meetings. In 2014/15, activist shareholders — in particular, New York City's Comptroller, responsible for the City's pension funds— used this route at dozens of US corporations, and many of these proxy access proposals passed. Since then, 60% of the S&P 500 corporations, and 400 U.S. corporations in total, have adopted proxy access bylaws under investor pressure.

3. A skeptical note: Why are proxy campaigns so costly?

Until now, however, proxy access has been used only once, and even then the challenger ultimately withdrew its candidate. Why? As explained above, the idea is that proxy access will make it much cheaper for an activist to propose a candidate, and hence alleviate the collective action problem. But let's take a closer look at the costs, and whether proxy access really reduces them.

Traditionally, an important expense in running proxy campaigns was mailing costs. These seem relatively minor now that challengers can make their materials available electronically (cf. rule 14a-16(l)) or solicit only a small number of large institutional investors, who now hold a large fraction of most corporations' shares. But challengers still need to buy a lot of lawyer time to comply with SEC requirements and to avoid fraud lawsuits under rule 14a-9. A successful campaign also tends to require lots of canvassing by proxy solicitors and campaigning with the help of public relations firms. After all, the insurgent must compete with the board, who buys the same services (including litigation) with the corporation's coffers. Costs for legal and other advice are rather independent of proxy access.

4. The Ideology of Proxy Access

If proxy access does not indeed reduce costs for "insurgent" shareholders, why would everyone fight about it? The answer is suggested by the following comment from Ted Mirvis of Wachtell, Lipton, Rosen, & Katz in response to the 2007 proposals:

> "Wars have many fronts. The battle lines in the fight between the director-centric and the shareholder-centric models of the world now once again include the SEC, as it considers whether to allow shareholders to use a company's proxy statement for director nominations."

Chapter 4. The Duty of Loyalty

This chapter begins our exploration of fiduciary duties. As previously mentioned, fiduciary duties originate in equity and comprise the duty of loyalty and the duty of care. This chapter focuses on the duty of loyalty; Chapter 5 considers the duty of care.

Both duties apply equally to directors and officers (*Gantler v. Stephens*, Del. 2009). Controlling stockholders are subject to fiduciary duties as well and generate some of the most important duty-of-loyalty cases (*cf. Sinclair* in this section and *Weinberger*, *MFW*, and *Delphi* in the M&A part of the course).

As a first approximation, the duties of care and loyalty target what their names imply: the duty of care demands that the fiduciary act with appropriate care, while the duty of loyalty demands that the fiduciary act loyally, i.e., guided by the interests of the principal. In other words, the former addresses simple mistakes, while the latter addresses conflicts of interest, i.e., self-dealing. Delaware courts vigilantly police self-dealing but are unreceptive to claims of honest mistakes.

◆ The controller's agreed share is the controller's percentage of the cash flow rights according to the corporation's charter and other relevant contracts.

(Minority) Shareholders' interests are most at risk in transactions between the corporation and its controllers, be it management or large shareholders. The risk is obvious: the controllers may attempt to extract more than their agreed share◆ of the corporation's value for themselves, at the expense of (minority) shareholders.

1. Some (not so) fictitious examples

Here are three typical ways controlling shareholders do it. I will illustrate using a fictitious oil company, OilCo, with a controlling stockholder, Mikhail. Mikhail owns 50% of OilCo, and 100% of another fictitious company, Honeypot.

> 1. The first thing Mikhail can do is to have OilCo sell its oil to Honeypot at below-market prices. For example, if the market price of oil is $16 per barrel, Mikhail might arrange for OilCo to sell its oil to Honeypot for $10. For every barrel of oil, this redistributes $3 from minority shareholders to Mikhail. Why? Because if OilCo had sold its oil on the market instead, it would have received $16 per barrel. These $16 would have been shared equally between Mikhail and the minority shareholders. Each would have received $8. But when OilCo instead sells to Honeypot for $10 per barrel, minority shareholders get only $5 (half of $10). The difference of $3 is

captured by Mikhail: per barrel of oil, he gets $5 as a shareholder of OilCo and $6 as the sole shareholder of Honeypot (because Honeypot buys for $10 and sells for $16, generating a $6 profit), or a total of $11. The use of artificially inflated or deflated prices to shift value from one company to another is called a **transfer pricing** scheme. It is also used for tax avoidance purposes.

2. Mikhail can also have OilCo issue new shares to himself or to Honeypot at low prices. For example, imagine that OilCo owns oil fields worth $100 m(illion), and that OilCo has one million shares outstanding. That means each share is worth $100 (assuming no transfer pricing scheme), and Mikhail's 50% stake and the 50% minority shares as a group each comprise 500,000 shares worth $50 million in total. Mikhail now has OilCo issue 100 million shares to himself at $0.01 per share for an overall price of $1 million. This means three things. First, OilCo is now worth $101 million: In addition to the $100 million oil field, it now has the $1 million cash that Mikhail put in for the new shares. Second, Mikhail now owns almost the entire company, owning 100.5 million out of 101 million shares (99.5%). Third, the transaction earned him $49.5 million: Before the transaction, Mikhail owned OilCo shares worth $50m (50% × $100m). After buying the new shares, Mikhail now owns shares worth $100.5m (99.5% × $101m). Thus, Mikhail spent $1m to increase his OilCo holding by $50.5m ($100.5m – $50m), generating a pure profit of $49.5m ($50.5m – $1m). Mikhail's gain is the minority shareholders' loss: they lost $49.5 million in this **dilution** of their share.

3. Finally, Mikhail can also dispense with the minority altogether by selling OilCo's assets to Honeypot for a low price. To wit, he could have OilCo sell its oil fields to Honeypot for less than their $100 million value. This is another transfer pricing scheme, but executed on OilCo's productive assets rather than its products, and hence also known as **asset stripping**. As with other transfer pricing schemes, it can also be done in reverse: Mikhail could have OilCo buy an asset from Honeypot at an inflated price.

None of these schemes is fictitious at all. For example, they are stylized versions of what Mikhail Khodorkovsky and all the other Russian oligarchs are said to have done to the oil companies they came to control in Russia in the 1990s. Russian corporate law erected barriers to such self-dealing. But corrupt, scared, or just plain incompetent courts breached those barriers. It is a vivid illustration of the importance of the general "legal infrastructure" for the enforcement of corporate law. See generally Bernard Black, Reinier Kraakman, & Anna Tarassova, *Russian Privatization and Corporate Governance: What Went Wrong?*, 52 STAN. L. REV. 1731 (2000).

2. The U.S. approach

Now back to the U.S., where we nowadays take a functioning "legal infrastructure" for granted. What protections does it offer against minority expropriation?

First, public corporations are prohibited from making loans to its directors or officers (section 13(k) of the Exchange Act, as amended by section 402 of the Sarbanes-Oxley Act of 2002). More importantly (because loans are only one form of self-dealing among many), public corporations must disclose all self-dealing transactions in an amount above $120,000 in their annual report (item 404 of the SEC's Regulation S-K). Managers or a controlling shareholder may choose to not comply with this rule, but only at the risk of becoming the target of an SEC enforcement action.

The only provision of the DGCL that explicitly addresses self-dealing is DGCL 144. On its face, DGCL 144 merely declares that transactions between the corporation and its officers and directors are *not* void or voidable *solely* because of the conflict of interest, *provided* the transaction fulfills *one* of the three conditions in subparagraphs (a)(1)-(3). This statutory text implies that transactions not fulfilling *either* of these conditions *are* automatically void or voidable. But the text leaves open the possibility that some conflicted transactions might be void or voidable even though they do fulfill one of the three conditions of DGCL 144(a)(1)-(3).

Notwithstanding, Delaware courts do treat the three conditions as individually sufficient and jointly necessary for the permissibility of self-dealing by directors and officers. That is, self-dealing by officers and directors is beyond judicial reproach if and only if it has been approved in good faith by a majority of fully informed, disinterested directors or shareholders, or it is otherwise shown to be "entirely fair." The courts do not derive this formulation from DGCL 144, however, but from "equitable principles." Moreover, *controlling shareholders* are subject to more stringent review: their self-dealing is always reviewed for "entire fairness;" approval by a "well-functioning committee of independent directors" or by fully informed disinterested shareholders merely shifts the burden of proof (subject to the recent doctrinal-transactional innovation of *Kahn v. MFW*, covered in the M&A part of the course).

What is "entire fairness"? It is not clear anybody knows. The Delaware Supreme Court essentially refuses to define it. In the authoritative words of *Weinberger* (covered in the M&A part below):

> The concept of fairness has two basic aspects: fair dealing and fair price. The former embraces questions of when the transaction was timed, how it was initiated, structured, negotiated, disclosed to the directors, and how the approvals of the directors and the stockholders were obtained. The latter aspect of fairness relates to the economic and financial considerations of the [transaction], including all ... elements that affect the intrinsic or inherent value of [the object of the transaction]. ... However, the test for fairness is not a bifurcated one as between fair dealing and price. All aspects of the issue must be examined as a whole since the question is one of entire fairness.
>
> —*Weinberger v. UOP*, 457 A.2d 701, 711 (Del. 1983).

Presumably the message to fiduciaries is: if you are self-interested, then you better pay top dollar and generally go out of your way to show you treated the corporation fairly (or, if you are a mere director or officer, you get absolution from the independent directors or shareholders).

Before diving into the details of this self-dealing jurisprudence, consider a preliminary question: why permit any self-dealing? Delaware law can be characterized as an attempt to differentiate self-dealing that expropriates shareholders, from self-dealing that does not. It is likely that courts will make mistakes, however, and that some expropriation will slip through the judicial cracks. For instance, the transactions at issue in *Sinclair* (the oil sales), *Weinberger*, and *Americas Mining* later in the book resemble the three Mikhail examples above. While they were ultimately caught, the controlling shareholders in these Delaware corporations must have thought they might get away with the expropriation. And sometimes, they arguably do, as in *Aronson* (which, viewed in a skeptical light, resembles the first Mikhail example above).

Questions

1. Why not seal those cracks by prohibiting all self-dealing? The potential harm from self-dealing is great. What is the redeeming benefit, if any?

A. Guth v. Loft (Del. 1939) [Pepsi]

Guth is the mother of all Delaware duty of loyalty cases. The decision introduces the basic idea that it is incumbent on the fiduciary to prove that the fiduciary acted "in the utmost good faith" (or, in modern parlance, with "entire fairness") to the corporation in spite of the fiduciary's conflict of interest. As mentioned above, approval by a majority of fully informed, disinterested directors or shareholders can absolve the fiduciary or at least shift the burden of proof. In *Guth*, however, the Court of Chancery had found that Guth had not obtained such approval from his board.

The decision deals with two separate aspects of Guth's behavior. The corporate resources that Guth used for his business, such as Loft's funds and personnel, clearly belonged to Loft, and there was little question that Guth had to compensate Loft for their use. The contentious part of the decision deals with a difficult line-drawing problem: which transactions come within the purview of the duty of loyalty in the first place?

Questions

1. Surely fiduciaries must retain the right to self-interested behavior in some corner of their life. Where is the line?

2. In particular, which business opportunities are "corporate opportunities" belonging to the corporation, and which are open to the fiduciaries to pursue for their own benefit? Cf. DGCL 122(17).

3. And why does it matter here, seeing that *some* of Guth's actions clearly were actionable self-dealing? Hint: Which remedy is available for which action?

5 A.2d 503

GUTH et al.

v.

LOFT, Inc.

Supreme Court of Delaware.
April 11, 1939.

[...]

For convenience, Loft Incorporated, will be referred to as Loft; the Grace Company, Inc., of Delaware, as Grace; and Pepsi-Cola Company, a corporation of Delaware, as Pepsi.

Loft filed a bill in the Court of Chancery against Charles G. Guth, Grace and Pepsi seeking to impress a trust in favor of the complainant upon all shares of the capital stock of Pepsi registered in the name of Guth and in the name of Grace (approximately 91% of the capital stock), to secure a transfer of those shares to the complainant, and for an accounting.

The cause was heard at great length by the Chancellor who, on September 17, 1938, rendered a decision in favor of the complainant in accordance with the prayers of the bill. Loft, Inc., v. Guth, Del.Ch., 2 A.2d 225. An interlocutory decree, and an interlocutory order fixing terms of stay and amounts of supersedeas bonds, were entered on October 4, 1938; and, thereafter, an appeal was duly prosecuted to this Court.

The essential facts, admitted or found by the Chancellor, briefly stated, are these: Loft was, and is, a corporation engaged in the manufacturing and selling of candies, syrups, beverages and foodstuffs, having its executive offices and main plant at Long Island City, New York. In 1931 Loft operated 115 stores largely located in the congested centers of population along the Middle Atlantic seaboard. While its operations chiefly were of a retail nature, its wholesale activities were not unimportant, amounting in 1931 to over $800,000. It had the equipment and the personnel to carry on syrup making operations, and was engaged in manufacturing fountain syrups to supply its own extensive needs. It had assets exceeding $9,000,000 in value, excluding goodwill; and from 1931 to 1935, it had sufficient working capital for its own cash requirements.

Guth, a man of long experience in the candy, chocolate and soft drink business, became Vice President of Loft in August, 1929, and its president in March 1930.

Grace was owned by Guth and his family. It owned a plant in Baltimore, Maryland, where it was engaged in the manufacture of syrups for soft drinks, and it had been supplying Loft with "Lady Grace Chocolate Syrup".

In 1931, Coca-Cola was dispensed at all of the Loft Stores, and of the Coca-Cola syrup Loft made large purchases, averaging over 30,000 gallons annually. The cost of the syrup was $1.48 per gallon. Guth requested the Coca-Cola Company to give Loft a jobber's discount in view of its large requirements of syrups which exceeded greatly the purchases of some other users of the syrup to whom such discount had been granted. After many conferences, the Coca-Cola Company refused to give the discount. Guth became incensed, and contemplated the replacement of the Coca-Cola beverage with some other cola drink. On May 19, 1931, he addressed a memorandum to V. O. Robertson, Loft's vice-president, asking "Why are we paying a full price for Coca-Cola? Can you handle this, or would you suggest our buying Pebsaco (Pepsi-Cola) at about $1.00 per gallon?" To this Robertson replied that Loft was not paying quite full price for Coca-Cola, it paying $1.48 per gallon instead of $1.60, but that it was too much, and that he was investigating as to Pepsi-Cola.

Pepsi-Cola was a syrup compounded and marketed by National Pepsi-Cola Company, controlled by one Megargel. The Pepsi-Cola beverage had been on the market for upwards of twenty five years, but chiefly in southern territory. It was possessed of a secret formula and trademark. This company, as it happened, was adjudicated a bankrupt on May 26, 1931, upon a petition filed on May 18, the day before the date of Guth's memorandum to Robertson suggesting a trial of Pepsi-Cola syrup by Loft.

[506] Megargel was not unknown to Guth. In 1928, when Guth had no connection with Loft, Megargel had tried unsuccessfully to interest Guth and one Hoodless, vice-president and general manager of a sugar company, in National Pepsi-Cola Company. Upon the bankruptcy of this company Hoodless, who apparently had had some communication with Megargel, informed Guth that Megargel would communicate with him, and Megargel did inform Guth of his company's bankruptcy and that he was in a position to acquire from the trustee in bankruptcy, the secret formula and trademark for the manufacture and sale of Pepsi-Cola.

In July, 1931, Megargel and Guth entered into an agreement whereby Megargel would acquire the Pepsi-Cola formula and trademark; would form a new corporation, with an authorized capital of 300,000 shares of the par value of $5, to which corporation Megargel would transfer the formula and trademark; would keep 100,000 shares for himself, transfer a like number to Guth, and turn back 100,000 shares to the company as treasury stock, all or a part thereof to be sold to provide working capital. By the agreement between the two Megargel was to receive $25,000 annually for the first six years, and, thereafter, a royalty of 2 1/2 cents on each gallon of syrup.

Megargel had no money. The price of the formula and trademark was $10,000. Guth loaned Megargel $12,000 upon his agreement to repay him out of the first $25,000 coming to him under the agreement between the two, and Megargel made a formal assignment to Guth to that effect. The $12,000 was paid to Megargel in this way: $5000 directly to Megargel by Guth, and $7,000 by Loft's certified check, Guth delivering to Loft simultaneously his two checks aggregating $7000. Guth also advanced $426.40 to defray the cost of incorporating the company. This amount and the sum of $12,000 were afterwards repaid to Guth.

Pepsi-Cola Company was organized under the laws of Delaware in August, 1931. The formula and trademark were acquired from the trustee in bankruptcy of National Pepsi-Cola Company, and its capital stock was distributed as agreed, except that 100,000 shares were placed in the name of Grace.

At this time Megargel could give no financial assistance to the venture directly or indirectly. Grace, upon a comparison of its assets with its liabilities, was insolvent. Only $13,000 of Pepsi's treasury stock was ever sold. Guth was heavily indebted to Loft, and, generally, he was in most serious financial straits, and was entirely unable to finance the enterprise. On the other hand, Loft was well able to finance it.

Guth, during the years 1931 to 1935 dominated Loft through his control of the Board of Directors. He has completely controlled Pepsi. Without the knowledge or consent of Loft's Board of Directors he drew upon Loft without limit to further the Pepsi enterprise having at one time almost the entire working capital of Loft engaged therein. He used Loft's plant facilities, materials, credit, executives and employees as he willed. Pepsi's payroll sheets were a part of Loft's and a single Loft check was drawn for both.

An attempt was made to keep an account of the time spent by Loft's workmen on Pepsi's enterprises, and in 1935, when Pepsi had available profits, the account was paid; but no charge was made by Loft as against Pepsi for the services rendered by Loft's executives, higher ranking office employees or chemist, nor for the use of its plant and facilities.

[...]

Guth claimed that he offered Loft the opportunity to take over the Pepsi-Cola enterprise, frankly stating to the directors that if Loft did not, he would; but that the Board declined because Pepsi-Cola had proved a failure, and that for Loft to sponsor a company to compete with Coca-Cola would cause trouble; that the proposition was not in line with Loft's business; that it was not equipped to carry on such business on an extensive scale;

and that it would involve too great a financial risk. Yet, he claimed that, in August, 1933, the Loft directors consented, without a vote, that Loft should extend to Guth its facilities and resources without limit upon Guth's guarantee of all advances, and upon Guth's contract to furnish Loft a continuous supply of syrup at a favorable price. The guaranty was not in writing if one was made, and the contract was not produced.

[...]

The Chancellor found that Guth had never offered the Pepsi opportunity to Loft; [...] that Guth's use of Loft's money, credit, facilities and personnel in the furtherance of the Pepsi venture was without the knowledge or authorization of Loft's directors; that Guth's alleged personal guaranty to Loft against loss resulting from the venture was not in writing, and otherwise was worthless; that no contract existed between Pepsi and Loft whereby the former was to furnish the latter with a constant supply of syrup for a definite time and at a definite price; that as against Loft's contribution to the Pepsi-Cola venture, the appellants had contributed practically nothing; that after the repayment of the sum of $12,000 which had been loaned by Guth to Megargel, Guth had not a dollar invested in Pepsi stock; that Guth was a full time president of Loft at an attractive salary, and could not claim to have invested [508] his services in the enterprise; that in 1933, Pepsi was insolvent; that Loft, until July, 1934, bore practically the entire financial burdens of Pepsi, but for which it must have failed disastrously to the great loss of Loft.

[...]

By the decree entered the Chancellor found, inter alia, that Guth was estopped to deny that opportunity of acquiring the Pepsi-Cola trademark and formula was received by him on behalf of Loft, and that the opportunity was wrongfully appropriated by Guth to himself; that the value inhering in and represented by the 97,500 shares of Pepsi stock standing in the name of Guth and the 140,000 shares standing in the name of Grace, were, in equity, the property of Loft; that the dividends declared and paid on the shares of stock were, and had been, the property of Loft; and that for all practical purposes Guth and Grace were one.

The Chancellor ordered Guth and Grace to transfer the shares of stock to Loft; [...]

LAYTON, Chief Justice, delivering the opinion of the Court:

In the Court below the appellants took the position that, on the facts, the complainant was entitled to no equitable relief whatever. In this Court, they seek only a modification of the Chancellor's decree, not a reversal of it. They now contend that the question is one of equitable adjustment based upon the extent and value of the respective contributions of the appellants and the appellee. This change of position is brought about, as it is said, because of certain basic fact findings of the Chancellor which are admittedly unassailable in this Court. The appellants accept the findings of fact; but they contend that the Chancellor's inferences from them were unwarrantable in material instances [...]

Corporate officers and directors are not permitted to use their position of trust and confidence to further their private interests. While technically not trustees, they stand in a fiduciary relation to the corporation and its stockholders. A public policy, existing through the years, and derived from a profound knowledge of human characteristics and motives, has established a rule that demands of a corporate officer or director, peremptorily and inexorably, the most scrupulous observance of his duty, not only affirmatively to protect the interests of the corporation committed to his charge, but also to refrain from doing anything that would work injury to the corporation, or to deprive it of profit or advantage which his skill and ability might properly bring to it, or to enable it to make in the reasonable and lawful exercise of its powers. The rule that requires an undivided and unselfish loyalty to the corporation demands that there shall be no conflict between duty and self-interest. The occasions for the determination of honesty, good faith and loyal conduct are many and varied, and no hard and fast rule can be formulated. The standard of loyalty is measured by no fixed scale.

If an officer or director of a corporation, in violation of his duty as such, acquires gain or advantage for himself, the law charges the interest so acquired with a trust for the benefit of the corporation, at its election, while it denies to the betrayer all benefit and profit. The rule, inveterate and uncompromising in its rigidity, does not rest upon the narrow ground of injury or damage to the corporation resulting from a betrayal of confidence, but upon a broader foundation of a wise public policy that, for the purpose of removing all temptation, extinguishes all possibility of profit flowing from a breach of the confidence imposed by the fiduciary relation. Given the relation between the parties, a certain result follows; and a constructive trust is the remedial device through which precedence of self is compelled to give way to the stern demands of loyalty. [...]

The rule, referred to briefly as the rule of corporate opportunity, is merely one of the manifestations of the general rule that demands of an officer or director the utmost good faith in his relation to the corporation which he represents.

It is true that when a business opportunity comes to a corporate officer or director in his individual capacity rather than in his official capacity, and the opportunity is one which, because of the nature of the enterprise, is not essential to his corporation, and is one in which it has no interest or expectancy, the officer or director is entitled to treat the opportunity as his own, and the corporation has no interest in it, if, of course, the officer or director has not wrongfully embarked the [511] corporation's resources therein. Colorado & Utah Coal Co. v. Harris et al., 97 Colo. 309, 49 P.2d 429; Lagarde v.

Anniston Lime & Stone Co., 126 Ala. 496, 28 So. 199; Pioneer Oil & Gas Co. v. Anderson, 168 Miss. 334, 151 So. 161; Sandy River R. Co. v. Stubbs, 77 Me. 594, 2 A. 9; Lancaster Loose Leaf Tobacco Co. v. Robinson, 199 Ky. 313, 250 S.W. 997. But, in all of these cases, except, perhaps, in one, there was no infidelity on the part of the corporate officer sought to be charged. In the first case, it was found that the corporation had no practical use for the property acquired by Harris. In the Pioneer Oil & Gas Co. case, Anderson used no funds or assets of the corporation, did not know that the corporation was negotiating for the oil lands and, further, the corporation could not, in any event have acquired them, because their proprietors objected to the corporation's having an interest in them, and because the corporation was in no financial position to pay for them. In the Stubbs case, the railroad company, desiring to purchase from Porter such part of his land as was necessary for its right of way, station, water-tank, and woodshed, declined to accede to his price. Stubbs, a director, made every effort to buy the necessary land for the company and failed. He then bought the entire tract, and offered to sell to the company what it needed. The company repudiated expressly all participation in the purchase. Later the company located its tracks and buildings on a part of the land, but could not agree with Stubbs as to damages or terms of the conveyance. Three and one-half years thereafter, Stubbs was informed for the first time that the company claimed that he held the land in trust for it. In the Lancaster Loose Leaf Tobacco Co. case, the company had never engaged in the particular line of business, and its established policy had been not to engage in it. The only interest which the company had in the burley tobacco bought by Robinson was its commissions in selling it on its floors, and these commissions it received. In the Lagarde case, it was said that the proprietorship of the property acquired by the Legardes may have been important to the corporation, but was not shown to have been necessary to the continuance of its business, or that its purchase by the Legardes had in any way impaired the value of the corporation's property. This decision is, perhaps, the strongest cited on behalf of the appellants. With deference to the Court that rendered it, a different view of the correctness of the conclusion reached may be entertained.

On the other hand, it is equally true that, if there is presented to a corporate officer or director a business opportunity which the corporation is financially able to undertake, is, from its nature, in the line of the corporation's business and is of practical advantage to it, is one in which the corporation has an interest or a reasonable expectancy, and, by embracing the opportunity, the self-interest of the officer or director will be brought into conflict with that of his corporation, the law will not permit him to seize the opportunity for himself. And, if, in such circumstances, the interests of the corporation are betrayed, the corporation may elect to claim all of the benefits of the transaction for itself, and the law will impress a trust in favor of the corporation upon the property, interests and profits so acquired. [...]

But, there is little profit in a discussion of the particular cases cited. In none of them are the facts and circumstances comparable to those of the case under consideration. The question is not one to be decided on narrow or technical grounds, but upon broad considerations of corporate duty and loyalty.

[...]

Duty and loyalty are inseparably connected. Duty is that which is required by one's station or occupation; is that which one is bound by legal or moral obligation to do or refrain from doing; and it is with [512] this conception of duty as the underlying basis of the principle applicable to the situation disclosed, that the conduct and acts of Guth with respect to his acquisition of the Pepsi-Cola enterprise will be scrutinized. Guth was not merely a director and the president of Loft. He was its master. It is admitted that Guth manifested some of the qualities of a dictator. The directors were selected by him. Some of them held salaried positions in the company. All of them held their positions at his favor. Whether they were supine merely, or for sufficient reasons entirely subservient to Guth, it is not profitable to inquire. It is sufficient to say that they either wilfully or negligently allowed Guth absolute freedom of action in the management of Loft's activities, and theirs is an unenviable position whether testifying for or against the appellants.

Prior to May, 1931, Guth became convinced that Loft was being unfairly discriminated against by the Coca-Cola Company of whose syrup it was a large purchaser, in that Loft had been refused a jobber's discount on the syrup, although others, whose purchases were of far less importance, had been given such discount. He determined to replace Coca-Cola as a beverage at the Loft stores with some other cola drink, if that could be accomplished. So, on May 19, 1931, he suggested an inquiry with respect to desirability of discontinuing the use of Coca-Cola, and replacing it with Pepsi-Cola at a greatly reduced price. Pepsi-Cola was the syrup produced by National Pepsi-Cola Company. As a beverage it had been on the market for over twenty-five years, and while it was not known to consumers in the area of the Loft stores, its formula and trademark were well established. Guth's purpose was to deliver Loft from the thraldom of the Coca-Cola Company, which practically dominated the field of cola beverages, and, at the same time, to gain for Loft a greater margin of profit on its sales of cola beverages. Certainly, the choice of an acceptable substitute for Coca-Cola was not a wide one, and, doubtless, his experience in the field of bottled beverages convinced him that it was necessary for him to obtain a cola syrup whose formula and trademark were secure against attack. Although the difficulties and dangers were great, he concluded to make the change. Almost simultaneously, National Pepsi-Cola Company, in which Megargel was predominant and whom Guth knew, went into bankruptcy; and Guth was informed that the long established Pepsi-Cola formula and trademark could be had at a small price. Guth, of course, was Loft; and Loft's determination to replace Coca-Cola with some other cola beverage in its many stores was practically co-incidental with the opportunity to acquire the Pepsi-Cola formula and trademark. This was the condition of affairs when Megargel approached Guth. Guth contended that his negotiation with Megargel in 1931 was but a continuation of a negotiation begun in 1928, when he had no connection with Loft; but the Chancellor found to the contrary, and his finding is accepted.

It is urged by the appellants that Megargel offered the Pepsi-Cola opportunity to Guth personally, and not to him as president of Loft. The Chancellor said that there was no way of knowing the fact, as Megargel was dead, and the benefit of his testimony could not be had; but that it was not important, for the matter of consequence was how Guth received the proposition.

It was incumbent upon Guth to show that his every act in dealing with the opportunity presented was in the exercise of the utmost good faith to Loft; and the burden was cast upon him satisfactorily to prove that the offer was made to him individually. Reasonable inferences, drawn from acknowledged facts and circumstances, are powerful factors in arriving at the truth of a disputed matter, and such inferences are not to be ignored in considering the acts and conduct of Megargel. He had been for years engaged in the manufacture and sale of a cola syrup in competition with Coca-Cola. He knew of the difficulties of competition with such a powerful opponent in general, and in particular in the securing of a necessary foothold in a new territory where Coca-Cola was supreme. He could not hope to establish the popularity and use of his syrup in a strange field, and in competition with the assured position of Coca-Cola, by the usual advertising means, for he, himself, had no money or resources, and it is entirely unbelievable that he expected Guth to have command of the vast amount of money necessary to popularize Pepsi-Cola by the ordinary methods. He knew of the difficulty, not to say impossibility, of inducing proprietors of soft drink establishments to use a cola drink utterly unknown [513] to their patrons. It would seem clear, from any reasonable point of view, that Megargel sought to interest someone who controlled an existing opportunity to popularize his product by an actual presentation of it to the consuming public. Such person was Guth, the president of Loft. It is entirely reasonable to infer that Megargel approached Guth as president of Loft, operating, as it did, many soft drink fountains in a most necessary and desirable territory where Pepsi-Cola was little known, he well knowing that if the drink could be established in New York and circumjacent territory, its success would be assured. Every reasonable inference points to this conclusion. What was finally agreed upon between Megargel and Guth, and what outward appearance their agreement assumed, is of small importance. It was a matter of indifference to Megargel whether his co-adventurer was Guth personally, or Loft, so long as his terms were met and his object attained.

Leaving aside the manner of the offer of the opportunity, certain other matters are to be considered in determining whether the opportunity, in the circumstances, belonged to

Loft; and in this we agree that Guth's right to appropriate the Pepsi-Cola opportunity to himself depends upon the circumstances existing at the time it presented itself to him without regard to subsequent events, and that due weight should be given to character of the opportunity which Megargel envisioned and brought to Guth's door.

The real issue is whether the opportunity to secure a very substantial stock interest in a corporation to be formed for the purpose of exploiting a cola beverage on a wholesale scale was so closely associated with the existing business activities of Loft, and so essential thereto, as to bring the transaction within that class of cases where the acquisition of the property would throw the corporate officer purchasing it into competition with his company. This is a factual question to be decided by reasonable inferences from objective facts.

[...]

The appellants suggest a doubt whether Loft would have been able to finance the project along the lines contemplated by Megargel, viewing the situation as of 1931. The answer to this suggestion is two-fold. The Chancellor found that Loft's net asset position at that time was amply sufficient to finance the enterprise, and that its plant, equipment, executives, personnel and facilities, supplemented by such expansion for the necessary development of the business as it was well able to provide, were in all respects adequate. The second answer is that Loft's resources were found to be sufficient, for Guth made use of no other to any important extent.

Next it is contended that the Pepsi-Cola opportunity was not in the line of Loft's activities which essentially were of a retail nature. It is pointed out that, in 1931, the retail stores operated by Loft were largely located in the congested areas along the Middle Atlantic Seaboard, that its manufacturing [514] operations were centered in its New York factory, and that it was a definitely localized business, and not operated on a national scale; whereas, the Megargel proposition envisaged annual sales of syrup at least a million gallons, which could be accomplished only by a wholesale distribution. Loft, however, had many wholesale activities. Its wholesale business in 1931 amounted to over $800,000. It was a large company by any standard. It had an enormous plant. It paid enormous rentals. Guth, himself, said that Loft's success depended upon the fullest utilization of its large plant facilities. Moreover, it was a manufacturer of syrups and, with the exception of cola syrup, it supplied its own extensive needs. The appellants admit that wholsesale distribution of bottled beverages can best be accomplished by license agreements with bottlers. Guth, president of Loft, was an able and experienced man in that field. Loft, then, through its own personnel, possessed the technical knowledge, the practical business experience, and the resources necessary for the development of the Pepsi-Cola enterprise.

[...]

It is urged that Loft had no interest or expectancy in the Pepsi-Cola opportunity. That it had no existing property right therein is manifest; but we cannot agree that it had no concern or expectancy in the opportunity within the protection of remedial equity. Loft had a practical and essential concern with respect to some cola syrup with an established formula and trademark. A cola beverage has come to be a business necessity for soft drink establishments; and it was essential to the success of Loft to serve at its soda fountains an acceptible five cent cola drink in order to attract into its stores the great multitude of people who have formed the habit of drinking cola beverages. When Guth determined to discontinue the sale of Coca-Cola in the Loft stores, it became, by his own act, a matter of urgent necessity for Loft to acquire a constant supply of some satisfactory cola syrup, secure against probable attack, as a replacement; and when the Pepsi-Cola opportunity presented itself, Guth having already considered the availability of the syrup, it became impressed with a Loft interest and expectancy arising out of the circumstances and the urgent and practical need created by him as the directing head of Loft.

As a general proposition it may be said that a corporate officer or director is entirely free to engage in an independent, competitive business, so long as he violates no legal or moral duty with respect to the fiduciary relation that exists between the corporation and himself. The appellants contend that no conflict of interest between Guth and Loft resulted from his acquirement and exploitation of the Pepsi-Cola opportunity. They maintain that the acquisition did not place Guth in competition with Loft any more than a manufacturer can be said to compete with a retail merchant whom the manufacturer supplies with goods to be sold. However true the statement, applied generally, may be, we emphatically dissent from the application of the analogy to the situation of the parties here. There is no unity between the ordinary manufacturer and the retailer of his goods. Generally, the retailer, if he [515] becomes dissatisfied with one supplier of merchandise, can turn to another. He is under no compulsion and no restraint. In the instant case Guth was Loft, and Guth was Pepsi. He absolutely controlled Loft. His authority over Pepsi was supreme. As Pepsi, he created and controlled the supply of Pepsi-Cola syrup, and he determined the price and the terms. What he offered, as Pepsi, he had the power, as Loft, to accept. Upon any consideration of human characteristics and motives, he created a conflict between self-interest and duty. He made himself the judge in his own cause. This was the inevitable result of the dual personality which Guth assumed, and his position was one which, upon the least austere view of corporate duty, he had no right to assume. Moreover, a reasonable probability of injury to Loft resulted from the situation forced upon it. Guth was in the same position to impose his terms upon Loft as had been the Coca-Cola Company. If Loft had been in servitude to that company with respect to its need for a cola syrup, its condition did not change when its supply came to depend upon Pepsi, for, it was found by the Chancellor, against Guth's contention, that he had not given Loft the protection of a contract which secured to it a constant supply of Pepsi-Cola syrup at any definite price or for any definite time.

It is useless to pursue the argument. The facts and circumstances demonstrate that Guth's appropriation of the Pepsi-Cola opportunity to himself placed him in a competitive position with Loft with respect to a commodity essential to it, thereby rendering his personal interests incompatible with the superior interests of his corporation; and this situation was accomplished, not openly and with his own resources, but secretly and with the money and facilities of the corporation which was committed to his protection.

[...]

Upon a consideration of all the facts and circumstances as disclosed we are convinced that the opportunity to acquire the Pepsi-Cola trademark and formula, goodwill and business belonged to the complainant, and that Guth, as its President, had no right to appropriate the opportunity to himself.

[...]

B. Sinclair Oil Corp. v. Levien (Del. 1971)

Questions

1. As we learned in *Guth* and the introductory notes, the standard of review for self-dealing — "utmost good faith" or "intrinsic fairness" or, nowadays, "entire fairness" — is demanding. It is, thus, extremely important to determine which transactions count as self-dealing. What is *Sinclair*'s answer?

2. Do you agree with it?

3. May *Sinclair*'s answer condone abuse of minority stockholders?

4. What would happen if *Sinclair* had accepted the plaintiff's broader view, not just in the short run but also in the long run (when a corporate group has time to restructure)?

280 A.2d 717 (1971)

SINCLAIR OIL CORPORATION, Defendant Below, Appellant,

v.

Francis S. LEVIEN, Plaintiff Below, Appellee.

Supreme Court of Delaware.

June 18, 1971.

Henry M. Canby, of Richards, Layton & Finger, Wilmington, and Paul W. Williams, Floyd Abrams and Eugene R. Scheiman of Cahill, Gordon, Sonnett, Reindel & Ohl, New York City, for appellant.

Richard F. Corroon, Robert K. Payson, of Potter, Anderson & Corroon, Leroy A. Brill of Bayard, Brill & Handelman, Wilmington, and J. Lincoln Morris, Edward S. Cowen and Pollock & Singer, New York City, for appellee.

WOLCOTT, C. J., CAREY, J., and CHRISTIE, Judge, sitting. [719]

WOLCOTT, Chief Justice.

This is an appeal by the defendant, Sinclair Oil Corporation (hereafter Sinclair), from an order of the Court of Chancery, 261 A.2d 911 in a derivative action requiring Sinclair to account for damages sustained by its subsidiary, Sinclair Venezuelan Oil Company (hereafter Sinven), organized by Sinclair for the purpose of operating in Venezuela, as a result of dividends paid by Sinven, the denial to Sinven of industrial development, and a breach of contract between Sinclair's wholly-owned subsidiary, Sinclair International Oil Company, and Sinven.

Sinclair, operating primarily as a holding company, is in the business of exploring for oil and of producing and marketing crude oil and oil products. At all times relevant to this litigation, it owned about 97% of Sinven's stock. The plaintiff owns about 3000 of 120,000 publicly held shares of Sinven. Sinven, incorporated in 1922, has been engaged in petroleum operations primarily in Venezuela and since 1959 has operated exclusively in Venezuela.

Sinclair nominates all members of Sinven's board of directors. The Chancellor found as a fact that the directors were not independent of Sinclair. Almost without exception, they were officers, directors, or employees of corporations in the Sinclair complex. By reason of Sinclair's domination, it is clear that Sinclair owed Sinven a fiduciary duty. Getty Oil Company v. Skelly Oil Co., 267 A.2d 883 (Del.Supr. 1970); Cottrell v. Pawcatuck Co., 35 Del. Ch. 309, 116 A.2d 787 (1955). Sinclair concedes this.

The Chancellor held that because of Sinclair's fiduciary duty and its control over Sinven, its relationship with Sinven must meet the test of intrinsic fairness. The [720] standard of intrinsic fairness involves both a high degree of fairness and a shift in the burden of proof. Under this standard the burden is on Sinclair to prove, subject to careful judicial scrutiny, that its transactions with Sinven were objectively fair. Guth v. Loft, Inc., 23 Del.Ch. 255, 5 A.2d 503 (1939); Sterling v. Mayflower Hotel Corp., 33 Del.Ch. 293, 93 A.2d 107, 38 A. L.R.2d 425 (Del.Supr.1952); Getty Oil Co. v. Skelly Oil Co., supra.

Sinclair argues that the transactions between it and Sinven should be tested, not by the test of intrinsic fairness with the accompanying shift of the burden of proof, but by the business judgment rule under which a court will not interfere with the judgment of a board of directors unless there is a showing of gross and palpable overreaching. Meyerson v. El Paso Natural Gas Co., 246 A.2d 789 (Del.Ch. 1967). A board of directors enjoys a presumption of sound business judgment, and its decisions will not be disturbed if they can be attributed to any rational business purpose. A court under such circumstances will not substitute its own notions of what is or is not sound business judgment.

We think, however, that Sinclair's argument in this respect is misconceived. When the situation involves a parent and a subsidiary, with the parent controlling the transaction and fixing the terms, the test of intrinsic fairness, with its resulting shifting of the burden of proof, is applied. Sterling v. Mayflower Hotel Corp., supra; David J. Greene & Co. v. Dunhill International, Inc., 249 A.2d 427 (Del.Ch.1968); Bastian v. Bourns, Inc., 256 A.2d 680 (Del.Ch.1969) aff'd. Per Curiam (unreported) (Del.Supr.1970). The basic situation for the application of the rule is the one in which the parent has received a benefit to the exclusion and at the expense of the subsidiary.

Recently, this court dealt with the question of fairness in parent-subsidiary dealings in Getty Oil Co. v. Skelly Oil Co., supra. In that case, both parent and subsidiary were in the business of refining and marketing crude oil and crude oil products. The Oil Import Board ruled that the subsidiary, because it was controlled by the parent, was no longer entitled to a separate allocation of imported crude oil. The subsidiary then contended that it had a right to share the quota of crude oil allotted to the parent. We ruled that the business judgment standard should be applied to determine this contention. Although the subsidiary suffered a loss through the administration of the oil import quotas, the parent gained nothing. The parent's quota was derived solely from its own past use. The past use of the subsidiary did not cause an increase in the parent's quota. Nor did the parent usurp a quota of the subsidiary. Since the parent received nothing from the subsidiary to the exclusion of the minority stockholders of the subsidiary, there was no self-dealing. Therefore, the business judgment standard was properly applied.

A parent does indeed owe a fiduciary duty to its subsidiary when there are parent-subsidiary dealings. However, this alone will not evoke the intrinsic fairness standard. This standard will be applied only when the fiduciary duty is accompanied by self-dealing — the situation when a parent is on both sides of a transaction with its subsidiary. Self-dealing occurs when the parent, by virtue of its domination of the subsidiary, causes the subsidiary to act in such a way that the parent receives something from the subsidiary to the exclusion of, and detriment to, the minority stockholders of the subsidiary.

We turn now to the facts. The plaintiff argues that, from 1960 through 1966, Sinclair caused Sinven to pay out such excessive dividends that the industrial development of Sinven was effectively prevented, and it became in reality a corporation in dissolution.

From 1960 through 1966, Sinven paid out $108,000,000 in dividends ($38,000,000 [721] in excess of Sinven's earnings during the same period). The Chancellor held that Sinclair caused these dividends to be paid during a period when it had a need for large amounts of cash. Although the dividends paid exceeded earnings, the plaintiff concedes that the payments were made in compliance with 8 Del.C. § 170, authorizing payment of dividends out of surplus or net profits. However, the plaintiff attacks these dividends on the ground that they resulted from an improper motive — Sinclair's need for cash. The Chancellor, applying the intrinsic fairness standard, held that Sinclair did not sustain its burden of proving that these dividends were intrinsically fair to the minority stockholders of Sinven.

Since it is admitted that the dividends were paid in strict compliance with 8 Del.C. § 170, the alleged excessiveness of the payments alone would not state a cause of action. Nevertheless, compliance with the applicable statute may not, under all circumstances, justify all dividend payments. If a plaintiff can meet his burden of proving that a dividend cannot be grounded on any reasonable business objective, then the courts can and will interfere with the board's decision to pay the dividend.

Sinclair contends that it is improper to apply the intrinsic fairness standard to dividend payments even when the board which voted for the dividends is completely dominated. In support of this contention, Sinclair relies heavily on American District Telegraph Co. [ADT] v. Grinnell Corp., (N.Y.Sup.Ct.1969) aff'd. 33 A.D.2d 769, 306 N.Y.S.2d 209 (1969). Plaintiffs were minority stockholders of ADT, a subsidiary of Grinnell. The plaintiffs alleged that Grinnell, realizing that it would soon have to sell its ADT stock because of a pending anti-trust action, caused ADT to pay excessive dividends. Because the dividend payments conformed with applicable statutory law, and the plaintiffs could not prove an abuse of discretion, the court ruled that the complaint did not state a cause of action. Other decisions seem to support Sinclair's contention. In Metropolitan Casualty Ins. Co. v. First State Bank of Temple, 54 S.W.2d 358 (Tex.Civ.App.1932), rev'd. on other grounds, 79 S.W.2d 835 (Sup.Ct. 1935), the court held that a majority of interested directors does not void a declaration of dividends because all directors, by necessity, are interested in and benefited by a dividend declaration. See, also, Schwartz v. Kahn, 183 Misc. 252, 50 N.Y.S. 2d 931 (1944); Weinberger v. Quinn, 264 A.D. 405, 35 N.Y.S.2d 567 (1942).

We do not accept the argument that the intrinsic fairness test can never be applied to a dividend declaration by a dominated board, although a dividend declaration by a dominated board will not inevitably demand the application of the intrinsic fairness standard. Moskowitz v. Bantrell, 41 Del.Ch. 177, 190 A.2d 749 (Del.Supr. 1963). If such a dividend is in essence self-dealing by the parent, then the intrinsic fairness standard is the proper standard. For example, suppose a parent dominates a subsidiary and its board of directors. The subsidiary has outstanding two classes of stock, X and Y. Class X is owned by the parent and Class Y is owned by minority stockholders of the subsidiary. If the subsidiary, at the direction of the parent, declares a dividend on its Class X stock only, this might well be self-dealing by the parent. It would be receiving something from the subsidiary to the exclusion of and detrimental to its minority stockholders. This self-dealing, coupled with the parent's fiduciary duty, would make intrinsic fairness the proper standard by which to evaluate the dividend payments.

Consequently it must be determined whether the dividend payments by Sinven were, in essence, self-dealing by Sinclair. The dividends resulted in great sums of money being transferred from Sinven to Sinclair. However, a proportionate share of this money was received by the minority shareholders of Sinven. Sinclair received nothing from Sinven to the exclusion of its [722] minority stockholders. As such, these dividends were not self-dealing. We hold therefore that the Chancellor erred in applying the intrinsic fairness test as to these dividend payments. The business judgment standard should have been applied.

We conclude that the facts demonstrate that the dividend payments complied with the business judgment standard and with 8 Del.C. § 170. The motives for causing the declaration of dividends are immaterial unless the plaintiff can show that the dividend payments resulted from improper motives and amounted to waste. The plaintiff contends only that the dividend payments drained Sinven of cash to such an extent that it was prevented from expanding.

The plaintiff proved no business opportunities which came to Sinven independently and which Sinclair either took to itself or denied to Sinven. As a matter of fact, with two minor exceptions which resulted in losses, all of Sinven's operations have been conducted in Venezuela, and Sinclair had a policy of exploiting its oil properties located in different countries by subsidiaries located in the particular countries.

From 1960 to 1966 Sinclair purchased or developed oil fields in Alaska, Canada, Paraguay, and other places around the world. The plaintiff contends that these were all opportunities which could have been taken by Sinven. The Chancellor concluded that Sinclair had not proved that its denial of expansion opportunities to Sinven was intrinsically fair. He based this conclusion on the following findings of fact. Sinclair made no real effort to expand Sinven. The excessive dividends paid by Sinven resulted in so great a cash drain as to effectively deny to Sinven any ability to expand. During this same period Sinclair actively pursued a company-wide policy of developing through its subsidiaries new sources of revenue, but Sinven was not permitted to participate and was confined in its activities to Venezuela.

However, the plaintiff could point to no opportunities which came to Sinven. Therefore, Sinclair usurped no business opportunity belonging to Sinven. Since Sinclair received nothing from Sinven to the exclusion of and detriment to Sinven's minority stockholders, there was no self-dealing. Therefore, business judgment is the proper standard by which to evaluate Sinclair's expansion policies.

Since there is no proof of self-dealing on the part of Sinclair, it follows that the expansion policy of Sinclair and the methods used to achieve the desired result must, as far as Sinclair's treatment of Sinven is concerned, be tested by the standards of the business judgment rule. Accordingly, Sinclair's decision, absent fraud or gross overreaching, to achieve expansion through the medium of its subsidiaries, other than Sinven, must be upheld.

Even if Sinclair was wrong in developing these opportunities as it did, the question arises, with which subsidiaries should these opportunities have been shared? No evidence indicates a unique need or ability of Sinven to develop these opportunities. The decision of which subsidiaries would be used to implement Sinclair's expansion policy was one of business judgment with which a court will not interfere absent a showing of gross and palpable overreaching. Meyerson v. El Paso Natural Gas Co., 246 A.2d 789 (Del.Ch.1967). No such showing has been made here.

Next, Sinclair argues that the Chancellor committed error when he held it liable to Sinven for breach of contract.

In 1961 Sinclair created Sinclair International Oil Company (hereafter International), a wholly owned subsidiary used for the purpose of coordinating all of Sinclair's foreign operations. All crude purchases by Sinclair were made thereafter through International.

On September 28, 1961, Sinclair caused Sinven to contract with International whereby Sinven agreed to sell all of its [723] crude oil and refined products to International at specified prices. The contract provided for minimum and maximum quantities and prices.

The plaintiff contends that Sinclair caused this contract to be breached in two respects. Although the contract called for payment on receipt, International's payments lagged as much as 30 days after receipt. Also, the contract required International to purchase at least a fixed minimum amount of crude and refined products from Sinven. International did not comply with this requirement.

Clearly, Sinclair's act of contracting with its dominated subsidiary was self-dealing. Under the contract Sinclair received the products produced by Sinven, and of course the minority shareholders of Sinven were not able to share in the receipt of these products. If the contract was breached, then Sinclair received these products to the detriment of Sinven's minority shareholders. We agree with the Chancellor's finding that the contract was breached by Sinclair, both as to the time of payments and the amounts purchased.

Although a parent need not bind itself by a contract with its dominated subsidiary, Sinclair chose to operate in this manner. As Sinclair has received the benefits of this contract, so must it comply with the contractual duties.

Under the intrinsic fairness standard, Sinclair must prove that its causing Sinven not to enforce the contract was intrinsically fair to the minority shareholders of Sinven. Sinclair has failed to meet this burden. Late payments were clearly breaches for which Sinven should have sought and received adequate damages. As to the quantities purchased, Sinclair argues that it purchased all the products produced by Sinven. This, however, does not satisfy the standard of intrinsic fairness. Sinclair has failed to prove that Sinven could not possibly have produced or someway have obtained the contract minimums. As such, Sinclair must account on this claim.

Finally, Sinclair argues that the Chancellor committed error in refusing to allow it a credit or setoff of all benefits provided by it to Sinven with respect to all the alleged damages. The Chancellor held that setoff should be allowed on specific transactions, e. g., benefits to Sinven under the contract with International, but denied an over all setoff against all damages claimed. We agree with the Chancellor, although the point may well be moot in view of our holding that Sinclair is not required to account for the alleged excessiveness of the dividend payments.

We will therefore reverse that part of the Chancellor's order that requires Sinclair to account to Sinven for damages sustained as a result of dividends paid between 1960 and 1966, and by reason of the denial to Sinven of expansion during that period. We will affirm the remaining portion of that order and remand the cause for further proceedings.

C. Hypo: Board Service?

Imagine you are the in-house lawyer for a real estate developer, Rosalind Franklin Broes. Broes is doing business through RFB Condominiums Inc. ("RFBC"), a Delaware corporation. Broes is RFBC's sole shareholder and president. You are technically an employee of RFBC. RFBC develops and administers condo complexes in the Midwestern United States, mainly in Michigan.

Broes now wants your opinion on the following issue. One of RFBC's bankers, John Cash of Big Bank, has asked Broes to join the board of another real estate developer, CIS Inc., also a Delaware corporation. CIS is an erstwhile competitor of RFBC. It has been in chapter 11 for the last two years, however, and lost or sold most of its properties and contracts during that time. When it emerges from bankruptcy next month, it will only have interests in Texas. Cash sits on CIS's creditor committee on behalf of Big Bank, a major creditor of CIS. Cash would like to get Broes's experience onto CIS's board.

Broes is concerned that service on CIS's board will expose her to conflicts of interest. She has shared these concerns with Cash. In Cash's view, the concerns are unfounded. After all, he, Cash, also has access to much confidential information from both CIS and RFBC in his role as their banker. Besides, he argues, CIS and RFBC will no longer be operating in the same areas. Lastly, even if CIS wanted to expand back into the Midwest, Cash points out that CIS would find it very difficult to do so under the restrictive post-bankruptcy loan covenants that prohibit most acquisitions or additional financing.

Broes is still worried though. She looked around the internet, and what she found did not reassure her. The most famous description of the duty of loyalty sounds rather ominous to her. It was penned by Judge Benjamin Cardozo, then Chief Judge of the New York Court of Appeals, in *Meinhard v. Salmon*, 249 N.Y. 458 (1928):

> Joint adventurers, like copartners, owe to one another, while the enterprise continues, the duty of the finest loyalty. Many forms of conduct permissible in a workaday world for those acting at arm's length, are forbidden to those bound by fiduciary ties. A trustee is held to something stricter than the morals of the market place. Not honesty alone, but the punctilio of an honor the most sensitive, is then the standard of behavior. As to this there has developed a tradition that is unbending and inveterate. Uncompromising rigidity has been the attitude of courts of equity when petitioned to undermine the rule of undivided loyalty by the 'disintegrating erosion' of particular

exceptions ... Only thus has the level of conduct for fiduciaries been kept at a level higher than that trodden by the crowd. It will not consciously be lowered by any judgment of this court.

Broes says she definitely does not want to sink to the "level ... trodden by the crowd," but she isn't quite sure what "the punctilio of an honor the most sensitive" demands of her.

Questions

1. Can she or can she not serve on CIS's board without getting into trouble?

2. What would you advise Broes to do?

Chapter 5. The Duty of Care

Is there room for liability — and thus judicial involvement — in corporate decision-making, outside of self-dealing? Applying the business judgment rule, Delaware courts hardly ever sanction managers and boards absent self-dealing. Nor do other states' courts. In a well-known case, the New York Supreme Court absolved American Express's board of liability even though they had forgone an $80 million tax benefit (in today's money) without any convincing countervailing benefit. Some have called this area of the law the "law of director non-liability."

This raises two questions: Why no liability? And if there truly is no liability, why not say so outright and save the expense and distraction of litigation?

Importantly, the cases in this area still involve conflicts of interest, albeit of a subtler kind than the outright financial or similarly strong conflicts giving rise to claims of self-dealing. Boards' and managers' interests diverge from shareholders' interests at least inasmuch as the former have to do all the work but surrender most of the benefits to the latter, incentive compensation notwithstanding. As you read the cases, you should be on the lookout for more specific conflicts.

A. Smith v. Van Gorkom (Del. 1985)

This is the one case where Delaware courts imposed monetary liability on disinterested directors for breach of the duty of care. It caused a storm. Liability insurance rates for directors skyrocketed. The Delaware legislature intervened by enacting DGCL 102(b)(7), which allows exculpatory charter provisions to eliminate damages for breaches of the duty of care (see next section). Such charter provisions are now standard. Even without them, however, it is unlikely that a Delaware court would impose liability on these facts today. The courts seem to have retrenched — not in their doctrine but in how they apply it. *Cf. Disney* below.

You should, therefore, read the case not as an exemplary application of the duty of care, but as a policy experiment that showed that corporate law practitioners and lawmakers regard monetary damages on these facts as undesirable. Why?

Background: the Acquisition Process (more in M&A, infra)

The case involves the acquisition of the Trans Union Corporation by Marmon Group, Inc. As is typical, the acquisition is structured as a merger. The acquired corporation (the "target") merges with the acquiror (the "buyer") or one of the buyer's subsidiaries. In the merger, shares in the target are extinguished. In exchange, target shareholders receive cash or other consideration (usually shares in the buyer).

Under most U.S. statutes such as DGCL 251, the merger generally requires a merger agreement between the buyer and the target to be approved by the boards and a majority of the shareholders of each corporation. This entails two important consequences.

First, the board controls the process because only the board can have the corporation enter into the merger agreement. This is one example of why it is at least misleading to call shareholders the "owners of the corporation."

Two, in public corporations, the requirement of shareholder approval means that several months will pass between signing the merger agreement and completion of the merger. This is the time it takes to convene the shareholder meeting and solicit proxies in accordance with the applicable corporate law and SEC proxy rules. Of course, many things can happen during this time. In particular, other potential buyers may appear on the scene.

Questions

1. According to the majority opinion, what did the directors do wrong? In other words, what should the directors have done differently? Why did the business judgment rule not apply?

2. What are the dissenters' counter-arguments?

3. How do you think directors in other companies reacted to this decision — what, if anything, did they most likely do differently after *Van Gorkom*?

488 A.2d 858 (1985)

Alden SMITH and John W. Gosselin, Plaintiffs Below, Appellants,

v.

Jerome W. VAN GORKOM, Bruce S. Chelberg, William B. Johnson,
Joseph B. Lanterman, Graham J. Morgan, Thomas P. O'Boyle, W.
Allen Wallis, Sidney H. Bonser, William D. Browder, Trans Union
Corporation, a Delaware corporation, Marmon Group, Inc., a
Delaware corporation, GL Corporation, a Delaware corporation, and
New T. Co., a Delaware corporation, Defendants Below, Appellees.

Supreme Court of Delaware.
Submitted: June 11, 1984.
Decided: January 29, 1985.
[...]

William Prickett (argued) and James P. Dalle Pazze, of Prickett, Jones, Elliott, Kristol &
Schnee, Wilmington, and Ivan Irwin, Jr. and Brett A. Ringle, of Shank, Irwin, Conant &
Williamson, Dallas, Tex., of counsel, for plaintiffs below, appellants.

Robert K. Payson (argued) and Peter M. Sieglaff of Potter, Anderson & Corroon,
Wilmington, for individual defendants below, appellees.

Lewis S. Black, Jr., A. Gilchrist Sparks, III (argued) and Richard D. Allen, of Morris,
Nichols, Arsht & Tunnell, Wilmington, for Trans Union Corp., Marmon Group, Inc., GL
Corp. and New T. Co., defendants below, appellees.

Before HERRMANN, C.J., and McNEILLY, HORSEY, MOORE and CHRISTIE, JJ.,
constituting the Court en banc. [863]

HORSEY, Justice (for the majority):

This appeal from the Court of Chancery involves a class action brought by shareholders of
the defendant Trans Union Corporation ("Trans Union" or "the Company"), originally
seeking rescission of a cash-out merger of Trans Union into the defendant New T
Company ("New T"), a wholly-owned subsidiary of the defendant, Marmon Group, Inc.
("Marmon"). Alternate relief in the form of damages is sought against the defendant

members of the Board of Directors of Trans Union, [864] New T, and Jay A. Pritzker and Robert A. Pritzker, owners of Marmon.[1]

Following trial, the former Chancellor granted judgment for the defendant directors by unreported letter opinion dated July 6, 1982.[2] Judgment was based on two findings: (1) that the Board of Directors had acted in an informed manner so as to be entitled to protection of the business judgment rule in approving the cash-out merger; and (2) that the shareholder vote approving the merger should not be set aside because the stockholders had been "fairly informed" by the Board of Directors before voting thereon. The plaintiffs appeal.

Speaking for the majority of the Court, we conclude that both rulings of the Court of Chancery are clearly erroneous. Therefore, we reverse and direct that judgment be entered in favor of the plaintiffs and against the defendant directors for the fair value of the plaintiffs' stockholdings in Trans Union, in accordance with *Weinberger v. UOP, Inc.*, Del.Supr., 457 A.2d 701 (1983).[3]

We hold: (1) that the Board's decision, reached September 20, 1980, to approve the proposed cash-out merger was not the product of an informed business judgment; (2) that the Board's subsequent efforts to amend the Merger Agreement and take other curative action were ineffectual, both legally and factually; and (3) that the Board did not deal with complete candor with the stockholders by failing to disclose all material facts, which they knew or should have known, before securing the stockholders' approval of the merger.

---

[1] The plaintiff, Alden Smith, originally sought to enjoin the merger; but, following extensive discovery, the Trial Court denied the plaintiff's motion for preliminary injunction by unreported letter opinion dated February 3, 1981. On February 10, 1981, the proposed merger was approved by Trans Union's stockholders at a special meeting and the merger became effective on that date. Thereafter, John W. Gosselin was permitted to intervene as an additional plaintiff; and Smith and Gosselin were certified as representing a class consisting of all persons, other than defendants, who held shares of Trans Union common stock on all relevant dates. At the time of the merger, Smith owned 54,000 shares of Trans Union stock, Gosselin owned 23,600 shares, and members of Gosselin's family owned 20,000 shares.

[2] Following trial, and before decision by the Trial Court, the parties stipulated to the dismissal, with prejudice, of the Messrs. Pritzker as parties defendant. However, all references to defendants hereinafter are to the defendant directors of Trans Union, unless otherwise noted.

[3] It has been stipulated that plaintiffs sue on behalf of a class consisting of 10,537 shareholders (out of a total of 12,844) and that the class owned 12,734,404 out of 13,357,758 shares of Trans Union outstanding.

I.

The nature of this case requires a detailed factual statement. The following facts are essentially uncontradicted:[4]

-A-

Trans Union was a publicly-traded, diversified holding company, the principal earnings of which were generated by its railcar leasing business. During the period here involved, the Company had a cash flow of hundreds of millions of dollars annually. However, the Company had difficulty in generating sufficient taxable income to offset increasingly large investment tax credits (ITCs). Accelerated depreciation deductions had decreased available taxable income against which to offset accumulating ITCs. The Company took these deductions, despite their effect on usable ITCs, because the rental price in the railcar leasing market had already impounded the purported tax savings.♦

♦ In other words, Transunion's "problem" was that it could not make full use of the available massive tax breaks. These tax breaks would reduce the corporate income tax. But Transunion benefitted from so many tax breaks that it was already not paying corporate income tax. The remaining tax breaks were thus "wasted," unless Transunion could persuade Congress to pay out those breaks in cash (i.e., to allow income taxes to be negative in this case -- from the Treasury to firms) or find other taxable income to use the tax breaks on.

In the late 1970's, together with other capital-intensive firms, Trans Union lobbied in Congress to have ITCs refundable in cash to firms which could not fully utilize the credit. During the summer of 1980, defendant Jerome W. Van Gorkom, Trans Union's Chairman and Chief Executive Officer, [865] testified and lobbied in Congress for refundability of ITCs and against further accelerated depreciation. By the end of August, Van Gorkom was convinced that Congress would neither accept the refundability concept nor curtail further accelerated depreciation.

Beginning in the late 1960's, and continuing through the 1970's, Trans Union pursued a program of acquiring small companies in order to increase available taxable income. In July 1980, Trans Union Management prepared the annual revision of the Company's Five Year Forecast. This report was presented to the Board of Directors at its July, 1980 meeting. The report projected an annual income growth of about 20%. The report also concluded that Trans Union would have about $195 million in spare cash between 1980 and 1985, "with the surplus growing rapidly from 1982 onward." The report referred to the ITC situation as a "nagging problem" and, given that problem, the leasing company "would still appear to be constrained to a tax breakeven." The report then listed four alternative uses of the projected 1982-1985 equity surplus: (1) stock repurchase; (2) dividend increases; (3) a major acquisition program; and (4) combinations of the above. The sale of Trans Union

---

[4] More detailed statements of facts, consistent with this factual outline, appear in related portions of this Opinion.

was not among the alternatives. The report emphasized that, despite the overall surplus, the operation of the Company would consume all available equity for the next several years, and concluded: "As a result, we have sufficient time to fully develop our course of action."

-B-

On August 27, 1980, Van Gorkom met with Senior Management of Trans Union. Van Gorkom reported on his lobbying efforts in Washington and his desire to find a solution to the tax credit problem more permanent than a continued program of acquisitions. Various alternatives were suggested and discussed preliminarily, including the sale of Trans Union to a company with a large amount of taxable income. [HS: The buyer could then merge with Transunion and, under applicable IRS rules and certain conditions, apply the tax credits of the former Transunion to the combined taxable income of the merged entities.]

Donald Romans, Chief Financial Officer of Trans Union, stated that his department had done a "very brief bit of work on the possibility of a leveraged buy-out."♦

This work had been prompted by a media article which Romans had seen regarding a leveraged buy-out by management. The work consisted of a "preliminary study" of the cash which could be generated by the Company if it participated in a leveraged buyout. As Romans stated, this analysis "was very first and rough cut at seeing whether a cash flow would support what might be considered a high price for this type of transaction."

On September 5, at another Senior Management meeting which Van Gorkom attended, Romans again brought up the idea of a leveraged buy-out as a "possible strategic alternative" to the Company's acquisition program. Romans and Bruce S. Chelberg, President and Chief Operating Officer of Trans Union, had been

♦ A leveraged buyout (LBO) is a purchase financed largely with debt. The debt is usually secured by the purchased corporation's assets. LBOs became frequent and spectacularly large in the 1980s. For the LBO to succeed post-acquisition, the target corporation must produce high and steady cash flows to service the high levels of debt incurred. Otherwise, the target will end up in bankruptcy. We will discuss these issues in much greater detail when we discuss Unocal later in the course.

working on the matter in preparation for the meeting. According to Romans: They did not "come up" with a price for the Company. They merely "ran the numbers" at $50 a share and at $60 a share with the "rough form" of their cash figures at the time. Their "figures indicated that $50 would be very easy to do but $60 would be very difficult to do under those figures." This work did not purport to establish a fair price for either the Company or 100% of the stock. It was intended to determine the cash flow needed to service the debt that would "probably" be incurred in a leveraged buyout, based on "rough calculations" without "any benefit of experts to identify what the limits were to that, and so forth." These computations were not considered extensive and no conclusion was reached.

At this meeting, Van Gorkom stated that he would be willing to take $55 per share for his own 75,000 shares. He vetoed the suggestion of a leveraged buy-out by Management, however, as involving a potential conflict of interest for Management. Van Gorkom, a certified public accountant and lawyer, had been an officer of Trans Union [866] for 24 years, its Chief Executive Officer for more than 17 years, and Chairman of its Board for 2 years. It is noteworthy in this connection that he was then approaching 65 years of age and mandatory retirement.

For several days following the September 5 meeting, Van Gorkom pondered the idea of a sale. He had participated in many acquisitions as a manager and director of Trans Union and as a director of other companies. He was familiar with acquisition procedures, valuation methods, and negotiations; and he privately considered the pros and cons of whether Trans Union should seek a privately or publicly-held purchaser.

Van Gorkom decided to meet with Jay A. Pritzker, a well-known corporate takeover specialist and a social acquaintance. However, rather than approaching Pritzker simply to determine his interest in acquiring Trans Union, Van Gorkom assembled a proposed per share price for sale of the Company and a financing structure by which to accomplish the sale. Van Gorkom did so without consulting either his Board or any members of Senior Management except one: Carl Peterson, Trans Union's Controller. Telling Peterson that he wanted no other person on his staff to know what he was doing, but without telling him why, Van Gorkom directed Peterson to calculate the feasibility of a leveraged buy-out at an assumed price per share of $55. Apart from the Company's historic stock market price,[5] and Van Gorkom's long association with Trans Union, the record is devoid of any competent evidence that $55 represented the per share intrinsic value of the Company.

Having thus chosen the $55 figure, based solely on the availability of a leveraged buy-out, Van Gorkom multiplied the price per share by the number of shares outstanding to reach a total value of the Company of $690 million. Van Gorkom told Peterson to use this $690 million figure and to assume a $200 million equity contribution by the buyer. Based on these assumptions, Van Gorkom directed Peterson to determine whether the debt portion of the purchase price could be paid off in five years or less if financed by Trans Union's cash flow as projected in the Five Year Forecast, and by the sale of certain weaker divisions

---

[5] The common stock of Trans Union was traded on the New York Stock Exchange. Over the five year period from 1975 through 1979, Trans Union's stock had traded within a range of a high of $39½ and a low of $24¼. Its high and low range for 1980 through September 19 (the last trading day before announcement of the merger) was $38¼-$29½.

identified in a study done for Trans Union by the Boston Consulting Group ("BCG study"). Peterson reported that, of the purchase price, approximately $50-80 million would remain outstanding after five years. Van Gorkom was disappointed, but decided to meet with Pritzker nevertheless.

Van Gorkom arranged a meeting with Pritzker at the latter's home on Saturday, September 13, 1980. Van Gorkom prefaced his presentation by stating to Pritzker: "Now as far as you are concerned, I can, I think, show how you can pay a substantial premium over the present stock price and pay off most of the loan in the first five years. * * * If you could pay $55 for this Company, here is a way in which I think it can be financed."

Van Gorkom then reviewed with Pritzker his calculations based upon his proposed price of $55 per share. Although Pritzker mentioned $50 as a more attractive figure, no other price was mentioned. However, Van Gorkom stated that to be sure that $55 was the best price obtainable, Trans Union should be free to accept any better offer. Pritzker demurred, stating that his organization would serve as a "stalking horse" for an "auction contest" only if Trans Union would permit Pritzker to buy 1,750,000 shares of Trans Union stock at market price which Pritzker could then sell to any higher bidder. After further discussion on this point, Pritzker told Van Gorkom that he would give him a more definite reaction soon.

[867] On Monday, September 15, Pritzker advised Van Gorkom that he was interested in the $55 cash-out merger proposal and requested more information on Trans Union. Van Gorkom agreed to meet privately with Pritzker, accompanied by Peterson, Chelberg, and Michael Carpenter, Trans Union's consultant from the Boston Consulting Group. The meetings took place on September 16 and 17. Van Gorkom was "astounded that events were moving with such amazing rapidity."

On Thursday, September 18, Van Gorkom met again with Pritzker. At that time, Van Gorkom knew that Pritzker intended to make a cash-out merger offer at Van Gorkom's proposed $55 per share. Pritzker instructed his attorney, a merger and acquisition specialist, to begin drafting merger documents. There was no further discussion of the $55 price. However, the number of shares of Trans Union's treasury stock to be offered to Pritzker was negotiated down to one million shares; the price was set at $38-75 cents above the per share price at the close of the market on September 19. At this point, Pritzker insisted that the Trans Union Board act on his merger proposal within the next three days, stating to Van Gorkom: "We have to have a decision by no later than Sunday [evening, September 21] before the opening of the English stock exchange on Monday morning." Pritzker's lawyer was then instructed to draft the merger documents, to be reviewed by Van Gorkom's lawyer, "sometimes with discussion and sometimes not, in the haste to get it finished."

On Friday, September 19, Van Gorkom, Chelberg, and Pritzker consulted with Trans Union's lead bank regarding the financing of Pritzker's purchase of Trans Union. The bank indicated that it could form a syndicate of banks that would finance the transaction. On the same day, Van Gorkom retained James Brennan, Esquire, to advise Trans Union on the legal aspects of the merger. Van Gorkom did not consult with William Browder, a Vice-President and director of Trans Union and former head of its legal department, or with William Moore, then the head of Trans Union's legal staff.

On Friday, September 19, Van Gorkom called a special meeting of the Trans Union Board for noon the following day. He also called a meeting of the Company's Senior Management to convene at 11:00 a.m., prior to the meeting of the Board. No one, except Chelberg and Peterson, was told the purpose of the meetings. Van Gorkom did not invite Trans Union's investment banker, Salomon Brothers or its Chicago-based partner, to attend.

Of those present at the Senior Management meeting on September 20, only Chelberg and Peterson had prior knowledge of Pritzker's offer. Van Gorkom disclosed the offer and described its terms, but he furnished no copies of the proposed Merger Agreement. Romans announced that his department had done a second study which showed that, for a leveraged buy-out, the price range for Trans Union stock was between $55 and $65 per share. Van Gorkom neither saw the study nor asked Romans to make it available for the Board meeting.

Senior Management's reaction to the Pritzker proposal was completely negative. No member of Management, except Chelberg and Peterson, supported the proposal. Romans objected to the price as being too low;[6] he was critical of the timing and suggested that consideration should be given to the adverse tax consequences of an all-cash deal for low-basis shareholders; and he took the position that the agreement to sell Pritzker one million newly-issued shares at market price would inhibit other offers, as would the prohibitions against soliciting bids and furnishing inside information [868] to other bidders. Romans argued that the Pritzker proposal was a "lock up" and amounted to "an agreed merger as opposed to an offer." Nevertheless, Van Gorkom proceeded to the Board meeting as scheduled without further delay.

Ten directors served on the Trans Union Board, five inside (defendants Bonser, O'Boyle, Browder, Chelberg, and Van Gorkom) and five outside (defendants Wallis, Johnson, Lanterman, Morgan and Reneker). All directors were present at the meeting, except

---

[6] Van Gorkom asked Romans to express his opinion as to the $55 price. Romans stated that he "thought the price was too low in relation to what he could derive for the company in a cash sale, particularly one which enabled us to realize the values of certain subsidiaries and independent entities."

O'Boyle who was ill. Of the outside directors, four were corporate chief executive officers and one was the former Dean of the University of Chicago Business School. None was an investment banker or trained financial analyst. All members of the Board were well informed about the Company and its operations as a going concern. They were familiar with the current financial condition of the Company, as well as operating and earnings projections reported in the recent Five Year Forecast. The Board generally received regular and detailed reports and was kept abreast of the accumulated investment tax credit and accelerated depreciation problem.

Van Gorkom began the Special Meeting of the Board with a twenty-minute oral presentation. Copies of the proposed Merger Agreement were delivered too late for study before or during the meeting.[7] He reviewed the Company's ITC and depreciation problems and the efforts theretofore made to solve them. He discussed his initial meeting with Pritzker and his motivation in arranging that meeting. Van Gorkom did not disclose to the Board, however, the methodology by which he alone had arrived at the $55 figure, or the fact that he first proposed the $55 price in his negotiations with Pritzker.

Van Gorkom outlined the terms of the Pritzker offer as follows: Pritzker would pay $55 in cash for all outstanding shares of Trans Union stock upon completion of which Trans Union would be merged into New T Company, a subsidiary wholly-owned by Pritzker and formed to implement the merger; for a period of 90 days, Trans Union could receive, but could not actively solicit, competing offers; the offer had to be acted on by the next evening, Sunday, September 21; Trans Union could only furnish to competing bidders published information, and not proprietary information; the offer was subject to Pritzker obtaining the necessary financing by October 10, 1980; if the financing contingency were met or waived by Pritzker, Trans Union was required to sell to Pritzker one million newly-issued shares of Trans Union at $38 per share.

Van Gorkom took the position that putting Trans Union "up for auction" through a 90-day market test would validate a decision by the Board that $55 was a fair price. He told the Board that the "free market will have an opportunity to judge whether $55 is a fair price." Van Gorkom framed the decision before the Board not as whether $55 per share was the highest price that could be obtained, but as whether the $55 price was a fair price that the stockholders should be given the opportunity to accept or reject.[8]

---

[7] The record is not clear as to the terms of the Merger Agreement. The Agreement, as originally presented to the Board on September 20, was never produced by defendants despite demands by the plaintiffs. Nor is it clear that the directors were given an opportunity to study the Merger Agreement before voting on it. All that can be said is that Brennan had the Agreement before him during the meeting.

[8] In Van Gorkom's words: The "real decision" is whether to "let the stockholders decide it" which is "all you are being asked to decide today."

Attorney Brennan advised the members of the Board that they might be sued if they failed to accept the offer and that a fairness opinion was not required as a matter of law.

Romans attended the meeting as chief financial officer of the Company. He told the Board that he had not been involved in the negotiations with Pritzker and knew nothing about the merger proposal until [869] the morning of the meeting; that his studies did not indicate either a fair price for the stock or a valuation of the Company; that he did not see his role as directly addressing the fairness issue; and that he and his people "were trying to search for ways to justify a price in connection with such a [leveraged buy-out] transaction, rather than to say what the shares are worth." Romans testified:

> I told the Board that the study ran the numbers at 50 and 60, and then the subsequent study at 55 and 65, and that was not the same thing as saying that I have a valuation of the company at X dollars. But it was a way — a first step towards reaching that conclusion.

Romans told the Board that, in his opinion, $55 was "in the range of a fair price," but "at the beginning of the range."

Chelberg, Trans Union's President, supported Van Gorkom's presentation and representations. He testified that he "participated to make sure that the Board members collectively were clear on the details of the agreement or offer from Pritzker;" that he "participated in the discussion with Mr. Brennan, inquiring of him about the necessity for valuation opinions in spite of the way in which this particular offer was couched;" and that he was otherwise actively involved in supporting the positions being taken by Van Gorkom before the Board about "the necessity to act immediately on this offer," and about "the adequacy of the $55 and the question of how that would be tested."

The Board meeting of September 20 lasted about two hours. Based solely upon Van Gorkom's oral presentation, Chelberg's supporting representations, Romans' oral statement, Brennan's legal advice, and their knowledge of the market history of the Company's stock,[9] the directors approved the proposed Merger Agreement. However, the Board later claimed to have attached two conditions to its acceptance: (1) that Trans Union reserved the right to accept any better offer that was made during the market test period;

---

[9] The Trial Court stated the premium relationship of the $55 price to the market history of the Company's stock as follows:

> * * * the merger price offered to the stockholders of Trans Union represented a premium of 62% over the average of the high and low prices at which Trans Union stock had traded in 1980, a premium of 48% over the last closing price, and a premium of 39% over the highest price at which the stock of Trans Union had traded any time during the prior six years.

and (2) that Trans Union could share its proprietary information with any other potential bidders. While the Board now claims to have reserved the right to accept any better offer received after the announcement of the Pritzker agreement (even though the minutes of the meeting do not reflect this), it is undisputed that the Board did not reserve the right to actively solicit alternate offers.

The Merger Agreement was executed by Van Gorkom during the evening of September 20 at a formal social event that he hosted for the opening of the Chicago Lyric Opera. Neither he nor any other director read the agreement prior to its signing and delivery to Pritzker.

* * *

On Monday, September 22, the Company issued a press release announcing that Trans Union had entered into a "definitive" Merger Agreement with an affiliate of the Marmon Group, Inc., a Pritzker holding company. Within 10 days of the public announcement, dissent among Senior Management over the merger had become widespread. Faced with threatened resignations of key officers, Van Gorkom met with Pritzker who agreed to several modifications of the Agreement. Pritzker was willing to do so provided that Van Gorkom could persuade the dissidents to remain on the Company payroll for at least six months after consummation of the merger.

Van Gorkom reconvened the Board on October 8 and secured the directors' approval of the proposed amendments — sight unseen. The Board also authorized the employment of Salomon Brothers, its investment [870] banker, to solicit other offers for Trans Union during the proposed "market test" period.

The next day, October 9, Trans Union issued a press release announcing: (1) that Pritzker had obtained "the financing commitments necessary to consummate" the merger with Trans Union; (2) that Pritzker had acquired one million shares of Trans Union common stock at $38 per share; (3) that Trans Union was now permitted to actively seek other offers and had retained Salomon Brothers for that purpose; and (4) that if a more favorable offer were not received before February 1, 1981, Trans Union's shareholders would thereafter meet to vote on the Pritzker proposal.

It was not until the following day, October 10, that the actual amendments to the Merger Agreement were prepared by Pritzker and delivered to Van Gorkom for execution. As will be seen, the amendments were considerably at variance with Van Gorkom's representations of the amendments to the Board on October 8; and the amendments placed serious constraints on Trans Union's ability to negotiate a better deal and withdraw from the Pritzker agreement. Nevertheless, Van Gorkom proceeded to execute what became the October 10 amendments to the Merger Agreement without conferring further with the Board members and apparently without comprehending the actual implications of the amendments.

* * *

Salomon Brothers' efforts over a three-month period from October 21 to January 21 produced only one serious suitor for Trans Union — General Electric Credit Corporation ("GE Credit"), a subsidiary of the General Electric Company. However, GE Credit was unwilling to make an offer for Trans Union unless Trans Union first rescinded its Merger Agreement with Pritzker. When Pritzker refused, GE Credit terminated further discussions with Trans Union in early January.

In the meantime, in early December, the investment firm of Kohlberg, Kravis, Roberts & Co. ("KKR"), the only other concern to make a firm offer for Trans Union, withdrew its offer under circumstances hereinafter detailed. [HS: KKR is one the oldest, largest, and most successful private equity / LBO firms.]

On December 19, this litigation was commenced and, within four weeks, the plaintiffs had deposed eight of the ten directors of Trans Union, including Van Gorkom, Chelberg and Romans, its Chief Financial Officer. On January 21, Management's Proxy Statement for the February 10 shareholder meeting was mailed to Trans Union's stockholders. On January 26, Trans Union's Board met and, after a lengthy meeting, voted to proceed with the Pritzker merger. The Board also approved for mailing, "on or about January 27," a Supplement to its Proxy Statement. The Supplement purportedly set forth all information relevant to the Pritzker Merger Agreement, which had not been divulged in the first Proxy Statement.

* * *

On February 10, the stockholders of Trans Union approved the Pritzker merger proposal. Of the outstanding shares, 69.9% were voted in favor of the merger; 7.25% were voted against the merger; and 22.85% were not voted.

II.

We turn to the issue of the application of the business judgment rule to the September 20 meeting of the Board.

[...]

Under Delaware law, the business judgment rule is the offspring of the fundamental principle, codified in 8 *Del.C.* § 141(a), that the business and affairs of a Delaware corporation are managed by or under its board of directors. *Pogostin v. Rice*, Del.Supr.,

480 A.2d 619, 624 (1984); *Aronson v. Lewis,* Del.Supr., 473 A.2d 805, 811 (1984); *Zapata Corp. v. Maldonado,* Del.Supr., 430 A.2d 779, 782 (1981). In carrying out their managerial roles, directors are charged with an unyielding fiduciary duty to the corporation and its shareholders. *Loft, Inc. v. Guth,* Del.Ch., 2 A.2d 225 (1938), *aff'd,* Del.Supr., 5 A.2d 503 (1939). The business judgment rule exists to protect and promote the full and free exercise of the managerial power granted to Delaware directors. *Zapata Corp. v. Maldonado, supra* at 782. The rule itself "is a presumption that in making a business decision, the directors of a corporation acted on an informed basis, in good faith and in the honest belief that the action taken was in the best interests of the company." *Aronson, supra* at 812. Thus, the party attacking a board decision as uninformed must rebut the presumption that its business judgment was an informed one. *Id.*

The determination of whether a business judgment is an informed one turns on whether the directors have informed themselves "prior to making a business decision, of all material information reasonably available to them." *Id.*

Under the business judgment rule there is no protection for directors who have made "an unintelligent or unadvised judgment." *Mitchell v. Highland-Western Glass,* Del.Ch., 167 A. 831, 833 (1933). A director's duty to inform himself in preparation for a decision derives from the fiduciary capacity in which he serves the corporation and its stockholders. [...] Since a director is vested with the responsibility for the management of the affairs of the corporation, he must execute that duty with the recognition that he acts on behalf of others. Such obligation does not tolerate faithlessness or self-dealing. But fulfillment of the fiduciary function requires more than the mere absence of bad faith or fraud. Representation of the financial interests of others imposes on a director an affirmative duty to protect those interests and to proceed with a critical eye in assessing information of the type and under the circumstances present here. [...]

Thus, a director's duty to exercise an informed business judgment is in [873] the nature of a duty of care, as distinguished from a duty of loyalty. Here, there were no allegations of fraud, bad faith, or self-dealing, or proof thereof. Hence, it is presumed that the directors reached their business judgment in good faith, *Allaun v. Consolidated Oil Co.,* Del. Ch., 147 A. 257 (1929), and considerations of motive are irrelevant to the issue before us.

The standard of care applicable to a director's duty of care has also been recently restated by this Court. In *Aronson, supra,* we stated:

> While the Delaware cases use a variety of terms to describe the applicable standard of care, our analysis satisfies us that under the business judgment rule director liability is predicated upon concepts of gross negligence. (footnote omitted)

473 A.2d at 812.

We again confirm that view. We think the concept of gross negligence is also the proper standard for determining whether a business judgment reached by a board of directors was an informed one.

In the specific context of a proposed merger of domestic corporations, a director has a duty under 8 *Del.C.* 251(b), along with his fellow directors, to act in an informed and deliberate manner in determining whether to approve an agreement of merger before submitting the proposal to the stockholders. Certainly in the merger context, a director may not abdicate that duty by leaving to the shareholders alone the decision to approve or disapprove the agreement. *See Beard v. Elster,* Del.Supr., 160 A.2d 731, 737 (1960). Only an agreement of merger satisfying the requirements of 8 *Del.C.* § 251(b) may be submitted to the shareholders under § 251(c). *See generally Aronson v. Lewis, supra* at 811-13; *see also Pogostin v. Rice, supra.*

It is against those standards that the conduct of the directors of Trans Union must be tested, as a matter of law and as a matter of fact, regarding their exercise of an informed business judgment in voting to approve the Pritzker merger proposal.

III.

[...]

the question of whether the directors reached an informed business judgment in agreeing to sell the Company, pursuant to the terms of the September 20 Agreement presents, in reality, two questions: (A) whether the directors reached an informed business judgment on September 20, 1980; and (B) if they did not, whether the directors' actions taken subsequent to September 20 were adequate to cure any infirmity in their action taken on September 20. We first consider the directors' September 20 action in terms of their reaching an informed business judgment.

-A-

On the record before us, we must conclude that the Board of Directors did not reach an informed business judgment on September 20, 1980 in voting to "sell" the Company for $55 per share pursuant to the Pritzker cash-out merger proposal. Our reasons, in summary, are as follows:

The directors (1) did not adequately inform themselves as to Van Gorkom's role in forcing the "sale" of the Company and in establishing the per share purchase price; (2) were uninformed as to the intrinsic value of the Company; and (3) given these circumstances, at a minimum, were grossly negligent in approving the "sale" of the Company upon two hours' consideration, without prior notice, and without the exigency of a crisis or emergency.

As has been noted, the Board based its September 20 decision to approve the cash-out merger primarily on Van Gorkom's representations. None of the directors, other than Van Gorkom and Chelberg, had any prior knowledge that the purpose of the meeting was to propose a cash-out merger of Trans Union. No members of Senior Management were present, other than Chelberg, Romans and Peterson; and the latter two had only learned of the proposed sale an hour earlier. Both general counsel Moore and former general counsel Browder attended the meeting, but were equally uninformed as to the purpose of the meeting and the documents to be acted upon.

Without any documents before them concerning the proposed transaction, the members of the Board were required to rely entirely upon Van Gorkom's 20-minute oral presentation of the proposal. No written summary of the terms of the merger was presented; the directors were given no documentation to support the adequacy of $55 price per share for sale of the Company; and the Board had before it nothing more than Van Gorkom's statement of his understanding of the substance of an agreement which he admittedly had never read, nor which any member of the Board had ever seen.

Under 8 *Del.C.* § 141(e), "directors are fully protected in relying in [875] good faith on reports made by officers." [...] The term "report" has been liberally construed to include reports of informal personal investigations by corporate officers, *Cheff v. Mathes*, Del.Supr., 199 A.2d 548, 556 (1964). However, there is no evidence that any "report," as defined under § 141(e), concerning the Pritzker proposal, was presented to the Board on September 20.[16] Van Gorkom's oral presentation of his understanding of the terms of the proposed Merger Agreement, which he had not seen, and Romans' brief oral statement of his preliminary study regarding the feasibility of a leveraged buy-out of Trans Union do not qualify as § 141(e) "reports" for these reasons: The former lacked substance because Van Gorkom was basically uninformed as to the essential provisions of the very document about which he was talking. Romans' statement was irrelevant to the issues before the Board since it did not purport to be a valuation study. At a minimum for a report to enjoy the status conferred by § 141(e), it must be pertinent to the subject matter upon which a board is called to act, and otherwise be entitled to good faith, not blind, reliance. Considering all of the surrounding circumstances — hastily calling the meeting without

---

[16] In support of the defendants' argument that their judgment as to the adequacy of $55 per share was an informed one, the directors rely on the BCG study and the Five Year Forecast. However, no one even referred to either of these studies at the September 20 meeting; and it is conceded that these materials do not represent valuation studies. Hence, these documents do not constitute evidence as to whether the directors reached an informed judgment on September 20 that $55 per share was a fair value for sale of the Company.

prior notice of its subject matter, the proposed sale of the Company without any prior consideration of the issue or necessity therefor, the urgent time constraints imposed by Pritzker, and the total absence of any documentation whatsoever — the directors were duty bound to make reasonable inquiry of Van Gorkom and Romans, and if they had done so, the inadequacy of that upon which they now claim to have relied would have been apparent.

The defendants rely on the following factors to sustain the Trial Court's finding that the Board's decision was an informed one: (1) the magnitude of the premium or spread between the $55 Pritzker offering price and Trans Union's current market price of $38 per share; (2) the amendment of the Agreement as submitted on September 20 to permit the Board to accept any better offer during the "market test" period; (3) the collective experience and expertise of the Board's "inside" and "outside" directors;[17] and (4) their reliance on Brennan's legal advice that the directors might be sued if they rejected the Pritzker proposal. We discuss each of these grounds *seriatim:*

(1)

A substantial premium may provide one reason to recommend a merger, but in the absence of other sound valuation information, the fact of a premium alone does not provide an adequate basis upon which to assess the fairness of an offering price. Here, the judgment reached as to the adequacy of the premium was based on a comparison between the historically depressed Trans Union market price and the amount of the Pritzker offer. Using market price as a basis for concluding that the premium adequately reflected the true value [876] of the Company was a clearly faulty, indeed fallacious, premise, as the defendants' own evidence demonstrates.

The record is clear that before September 20, Van Gorkom and other members of Trans Union's Board knew that the market had consistently undervalued the worth of Trans Union's stock, despite steady increases in the Company's operating income in the seven years preceding the merger. The Board related this occurrence in large part to Trans Union's inability to use its ITCs as previously noted. Van Gorkom testified that he did not believe the market price accurately reflected Trans Union's true worth; and several of the directors testified that, as a general rule, most chief executives think that the market undervalues their companies' stock. Yet, on September 20, Trans Union's Board

---

[17] We reserve for discussion under Part III hereof, the defendants' contention that their judgment, reached on September 20, if not then informed became informed by virtue of their "review" of the Agreement on October 8 and January 26.

apparently believed that the market stock price accurately reflected the value of the Company for the purpose of determining the adequacy of the premium for its sale.

In the Proxy Statement, however, the directors reversed their position. There, they stated that, although the earnings prospects for Trans Union were "excellent," they found no basis for believing that this would be reflected in future stock prices. With regard to past trading, the Board stated that the prices at which the Company's common stock had traded in recent years did not reflect the "inherent" value of the Company. But having referred to the "inherent" value of Trans Union, the directors ascribed no number to it. Moreover, nowhere did they disclose that they had no basis on which to fix "inherent" worth beyond an impressionistic reaction to the premium over market and an unsubstantiated belief that the value of the assets was "significantly greater" than book value. By their own admission they could not rely on the stock price as an accurate measure of value. Yet, also by their own admission, the Board members assumed that Trans Union's market price was adequate to serve as a basis upon which to assess the adequacy of the premium for purposes of the September 20 meeting.

The parties do not dispute that a publicly-traded stock price is solely a measure of the value of a minority position and, thus, market price represents only the value of a single share. Nevertheless, on September 20, the Board assessed the adequacy of the premium over market, offered by Pritzker, solely by comparing it with Trans Union's current and historical stock price. (*See supra* note 5 at 866.)

Indeed, as of September 20, the Board had no other information on which to base a determination of the intrinsic value of Trans Union as a going concern. As of September 20, the Board had made no evaluation of the Company designed to value the entire enterprise, nor had the Board ever previously considered selling the Company or consenting to a buy-out merger. Thus, the adequacy of a premium is indeterminate unless it is assessed in terms of other competent and sound valuation information that reflects the value of the particular business.

Despite the foregoing facts and circumstances, there was no call by the Board, either on September 20 or thereafter, for any valuation study or documentation of the $55 price per share as a measure of the fair value of the Company in a cash-out context. It is undisputed that the major asset of Trans Union was its cash flow. Yet, at no time did the Board call for a valuation study taking into account that highly significant element of the Company's assets.

We do not imply that an outside valuation study is essential to support an informed business judgment; nor do we state that fairness opinions by independent investment bankers are required as a matter of law. Often insiders familiar with the business of a going concern are in a better position than are outsiders to gather relevant information; and under appropriate circumstances, such directors may be fully protected in relying in good faith upon the valuation reports of their management. [877] *See 8 Del.C.* § 141(e). *See also Cheff v. Mathes, supra.*

Here, the record establishes that the Board did not request its Chief Financial Officer, Romans, to make any valuation study or review of the proposal to determine the adequacy of $55 per share for sale of the Company. On the record before us: The Board rested on Romans' elicited response that the $55 figure was within a "fair price range" within the context of a leveraged buy-out. No director sought any further information from Romans. No director asked him why he put $55 at the bottom of his range. No director asked Romans for any details as to his study, the reason why it had been undertaken or its depth. No director asked to see the study; and no director asked Romans whether Trans Union's finance department could do a fairness study within the remaining 36-hour[18] period available under the Pritzker offer.

Had the Board, or any member, made an inquiry of Romans, he presumably would have responded as he testified: that his calculations were rough and preliminary; and, that the study was not designed to determine the fair value of the Company, but rather to assess the feasibility of a leveraged buy-out financed by the Company's projected cash flow, making certain assumptions as to the purchaser's borrowing needs. Romans would have presumably also informed the Board of his view, and the widespread view of Senior Management, that the timing of the offer was wrong and the offer inadequate.

The record also establishes that the Board accepted without scrutiny Van Gorkom's representation as to the fairness of the $55 price per share for sale of the Company — a subject that the Board had never previously considered. The Board thereby failed to discover that Van Gorkom had suggested the $55 price to Pritzker and, most crucially, that Van Gorkom had arrived at the $55 figure based on calculations designed solely to determine the feasibility of a leveraged buy-out.[19] No questions were raised either as to

---

[18] Romans' department study was not made available to the Board until circulation of Trans Union's Supplementary Proxy Statement and the Board's meeting of January 26, 1981, on the eve of the shareholder meeting; and, as has been noted, the study has never been produced for inclusion in the record in this case.

[19] As of September 20 the directors did not know: that Van Gorkom had arrived at the $55 figure alone, and subjectively, as the figure to be used by Controller Peterson in creating a feasible structure for a leveraged buy-out by a prospective purchaser; that Van Gorkom had not sought advice, information or assistance from either inside or outside Trans Union directors as to the value of the Company as an entity or the fair price per share for 100% of its stock; that Van Gorkom had not consulted with the Company's investment bankers or other financial analysts; that Van Gorkom had not consulted with or confided in any officer or director of the Company except Chelberg; and that Van Gorkom had deliberately chosen

the tax implications of a cash-out merger or how the price for the one million share option granted Pritzker was calculated.

We do not say that the Board of Directors was not entitled to give some credence to Van Gorkom's representation that $55 was an adequate or fair price. Under § 141(e), the directors were entitled to rely upon their chairman's opinion of value and adequacy, provided that such opinion was reached on a sound basis. Here, the issue is whether the directors informed themselves as to all information that was reasonably available to them. Had they done so, they would have learned of the source and derivation of the $55 price and could not reasonably have relied thereupon in good faith.

None of the directors, Management or outside, were investment bankers or financial analysts. Yet the Board did not consider recessing the meeting until a later hour that day (or requesting an extension of Pritzker's Sunday evening deadline) to give it time to elicit more information as to the sufficiency of the offer, either from [878] inside Management (in particular Romans) or from Trans Union's own investment banker, Salomon Brothers, whose Chicago specialist in merger and acquisitions was known to the Board and familiar with Trans Union's affairs.

Thus, the record compels the conclusion that on September 20 the Board lacked valuation information adequate to reach an informed business judgment as to the fairness of $55 per share for sale of the Company.[20]

(2)

This brings us to the post-September 20 "market test" upon which the defendants ultimately rely to confirm the reasonableness of their September 20 decision to accept the Pritzker proposal. In this connection, the directors present a two-part argument: (a) that by making a "market test" of Pritzker's $55 per share offer a condition of their September 20 decision to accept his offer, they cannot be found to have acted impulsively or in an uninformed manner on September 20; and (b) that the adequacy of the $17 premium for sale of the Company was conclusively established over the following 90 to 120 days by the most reliable evidence available — the marketplace. Thus, the defendants impliedly contend that the "market test" eliminated the need for the Board to perform any other form of fairness test either on September 20, or thereafter.

---

to ignore the advice and opinion of the members of his Senior Management group regarding the adequacy of the $55 price.

[20] For a far more careful and reasoned approach taken by another board of directors faced with the pressures of a hostile tender offer, see *Pogostin v. Rice, supra* at 623-627.

Again, the facts of record do not support the defendants' argument. There is no evidence: (a) that the Merger Agreement was effectively amended to give the Board freedom to put Trans Union up for auction sale to the highest bidder; or (b) that a public auction was in fact permitted to occur. The minutes of the Board meeting make no reference to any of this. Indeed, the record compels the conclusion that the directors had no rational basis for expecting that a market test was attainable, given the terms of the Agreement as executed during the evening of September 20. [...]

Van Gorkom, conceding that he never read the Agreement, stated that he was relying upon his understanding that, under corporate law, directors always have an inherent right, as well as a fiduciary duty, to accept a better offer notwithstanding an existing contractual commitment by the Board. (See the discussion *infra*, part III B(3) at p. 55.)

The defendant directors assert that they "insisted" upon including two amendments to the Agreement, thereby permitting a market test: (1) to give Trans Union the right to accept a better offer; and (2) to reserve to Trans Union the right to distribute proprietary information on the Company to alternative bidders. Yet, the defendants concede that they did not seek to amend the Agreement to permit Trans Union to solicit competing offers.

Several of Trans Union's outside directors resolutely maintained that the Agreement as submitted was approved on the understanding that, "if we got a better deal, we had a right to take it." Director Johnson so testified; but he then added, "And if they didn't put that in the agreement, then the management did not carry out the conclusion of the Board. And I just don't know whether they did or not." The only clause in the Agreement as finally executed to which the defendants can point as "keeping the door open" is the following underlined statement found in subparagraph (a) of section 2.03 of the Merger Agreement as executed:

> The Board of Directors shall recommend to the stockholders of Trans Union that they approve and adopt the Merger Agreement ("the stockholders' approval') and to use its best efforts to obtain the requisite votes therefor. *GL acknowledges that Trans Union directors may have a competing fiduciary obligation to the shareholders under certain circumstances.*

Clearly, this language on its face cannot be construed as incorporating either of the two "conditions" described above: either the right to accept a better offer or the right to distribute proprietary information to third parties. The logical witness for the defendants to call to confirm their construction of this clause of the Agreement would have been Trans Union's outside attorney, James Brennan. The defendants' failure, without explanation, to call this witness again permits the logical inference that his testimony would not have been helpful to them. The further fact that the directors adjourned, rather than recessed,